OPERA

FOR BEGINNERS

BY RON DAVID
ILLUSTRATED BY PAUL GORDON

Writers and Readers

WRITERS AND READERS PUBLISHING, INC.

P.O. Box 461, Village Station
New York, NY 10014

Writers and Readers Limited
9 Cynthia Street
London N1 9JF
England
•

A Writers and Readers Documentary Comic Book
Copyright © 1995
ISBN # 0-86316-086-7
1 2 3 4 5 6 7 8 9 0

Manufactured in the United States of America

Beginners Documentary Comic Books are published by Writers and
Readers Publishing, Inc. Its trademark, consisting of the words "For
Beginners, Writers and Readers Documentary Comic Books" and the
Writers and Readers logo, is registered in the U. S. Patent and
Trademark Office and in other countries.

edications

To the two women who protect me

◆ To my sexy voodoo wife who works out at Geraldo's gym and vows to kick the buns of anyone who messes with me.

◆ To my sexy Lebanese mother, who loves life, talks dirty, laughs like a mighty cloud of joy.

And to two women who are no longer in the touchable part of my life

◆ To my...other mother...the first thing she said to me was, "I know Susan can't cook but if you give her a chance..." (Dear Mom: You were wrong; she still can't cook.)

◆ To Patti (You can't be gone; I see you, or some part of you, everywhere.)

Ron

To Ruth and Eric, with every good wish.

To everyone who's ever sung in a shower.

Paul

TABLE OF CONTENTS

Introduction: The FAT LADY Overture..1

Act One: Opera HISTORY & COMPOSERS

Scene 1. OPERA'S PRE-OPERATIC ROOTS: 10

Scene 2. OPERA'S EARLY COMPOSERS: 1600-1800................................18

Scene 3. The 'BEL CANTO' COMPOSERS: 3 Geniuses...or 3 Stooges?..............28

Scene 4. VERDI: "Charley the Tuna" 35

Scene 5. WAGNER: Genius of MusicDrama or Boring Megalomaniac 38

Scene 6. FRENCH DUDES 43

Scene 7. ITALIAN 'VERISMO': "True-to-Life Opera".....................................46

Scene 8. RUSSIAN & SLAVIC OPERA..49

Scene 9. 20th CENTURY...50

Act Two: Opera SINGERS 57

Scene 10. The OPERATIC VOICE 58
Scene 11. The CASTRATI 62
Scene 12. B.C. (Before CARUSO) 68
Scene 13. Mr. CARUSO 76
Scene 14. A.C. (After CARUSO) 81
Scene 15. P.C. (Post CALLAS) 87

Act Three: LISTENING to Opera 101

Scene 16. A List of Miraculous Singers 113

Act Four: 'Listener-Friendly' OPERAS 123

Curtain Calls: 156
    The Intellectual Approach
    The Future of Opera

Discography 160
Resources 162
Glossary 163
Bibliography 164
Index 165

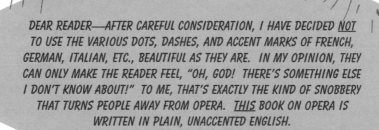

DEAR READER—AFTER CAREFUL CONSIDERATION, I HAVE DECIDED _NOT_ TO USE THE VARIOUS DOTS, DASHES, AND ACCENT MARKS OF FRENCH, GERMAN, ITALIAN, ETC., BEAUTIFUL AS THEY ARE. IN MY OPINION, THEY CAN ONLY MAKE THE READER FEEL, "OH, GOD! THERE'S SOMETHING ELSE I DON'T KNOW ABOUT!" TO ME, THAT'S EXACTLY THE KIND OF SNOBBERY THAT TURNS PEOPLE AWAY FROM OPERA. _THIS_ BOOK ON OPERA IS WRITTEN IN PLAIN, UNACCENTED ENGLISH.

$\mathcal{T}$ have many things I want to tell you,
or just one, but it is immense as the sea...

Mimi to Rudolfo
Act 4: PUCCINI'S *LA BOHÉME*

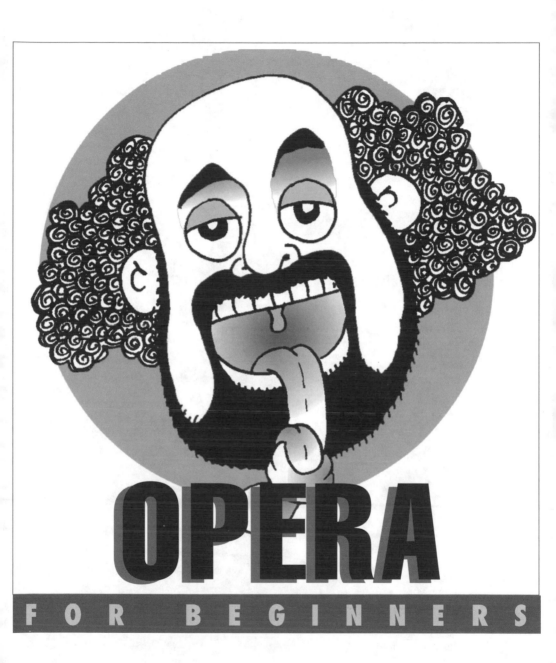

OPERA

FOR BEGINNERS

"THIS IS MY SECOND OPERA...

FAT LADY SANG.

DESPISED

IT!"

Steward Copeland,
drummer for THE POLICE
(the rock group, not
the Dudes in Blue)

THE FAT LADY *Overture*

Why do so many of you smart, suave, sexy people HATE Opera?

Because (you <u>think</u>) it's snobby, pretentious, uptight, lily white museum music...and all that other Republican baloney! (Enough about you!)

Me? If you must know the truth, in Detroit where I grew up, there weren't a hell of a lot of Opera houses. I was brought up on Little Richard, Bo Diddley, Elvis the Pelvis, the Drifters, Platters, Ella, Sinatra, Miles, Coltrane, Mahalia, Beatles, Stones, Aretha . . . in other words . . .

...**REAL** music!

Which is why I'm the perfect person to introduce you to Opera.

BESIDES: ALL THE OTHER INTROS TO OPERA ARE USELESS.

1

Q Why are most introductory books on Opera useless?

(And what makes this one any different?)

A Every Intro to Opera I've come across seemed to be written by a prissy little toad who was "born" listening to Opera. If the supernatural dumbness of that doesn't strike you right off, imagine if (for example) you spoke only English and wanted to learn Spanish. Would you get a teacher who spoke <u>only</u> Spanish?

Of course you wouldn't! You'd need a teacher who spoke <u>both</u> languages! People who were born listening to Opera have no idea what it's like to come to it from the outside. They don't speak our language—not in words, experiences, or emotions.

THE ARIA

MY OLD SEMANTICS TEACHER'D SAY THAT THEY HAVE DIFFERENT "REFERENTS" THAN WE DO: THE SAME WORDS HAVE SUCH DIFFERENT MEANINGS TO US AND THEM THAT WE REALLY ARE SPEAKING DIFFERENT LANGUAGES.

That, dudes, is why a Motor City saddle-tramp like myself is surely the ideal guide to the world of high-notes, prima donnas, and that god among Tenors...

..*Luciano Pepperoni!*

If this were an Opera, we'd swear eternal brotherhood, sing a rousing duet, jump on our fake horses, and take off after the **FAT LADY...**

AND, HONEY, I WOULD HIT A HIGHNOTE THAT WOULD MAKE YOU LOSE YOUR MORALS IN THE MIDDLE OF CENTRAL PARK!

Enough monkey beeswax!
Itza time to poppa the Question...

WHAT EXACTLY IS Opera?

"Opera is Music-Drama."
RICHARD WAGNER [1813-83]

"Opera is when a guy gets stabbed in the back and instead of bleeding, he sings."

ED GARDNER [1905-63]

Actually, Opera is two things:
Technically, Opera is a Drama in which the actors sing all or most of the dialogue. A Stage Play set to Music.

Unless you hate it.

When people say, "I hate Opera," they don't mean, "I hate Stage Plays set to Music"—the same people tell you how much they dug <u>Phantom of the Opera</u> or <u>X</u> or <u>Porgy</u> & <u>Bess</u>. They generally mean, "I hate fat ladies with loud, screechy voices."

So, you don't hate Opera. You hate . . .

> **THIS ISN'T NIT-PICKIN', IT'S AN IMPORTANT DISTINCTION**

YOU hate...

Opera SINGERS!

What can I tell you? In many cases, you're right! Some Opera singers really stink. (Remind me to tell you later why bad Opera singing is a lot like bad s-e-x.) You think you hate bad singers! LaScala Opera House in Milan, Italy is famous for having the hippest, baddest audience in Opera...

One evening a tenor appearing at LaScala in Verdi's *Il Trovatore* sang the flashy aria "Di quella pira." When he finished, the audience requested an encore, so the proud tenor sang the aria again. When he finished the encore, the ornery La Scala fans demanded *another* encore! The tenor was feeling like the Son of Caruso until one of the Opera lovers spilla-da-beanz:

"YOU'RE GOING TO KEEP SINGING IT UNTIL YOU GET IT RIGHT!"

There are few things as hideous as a bad Opera singer. Stick around: I'll guide you _around_ the bad ones and <u>to</u> great ones.

"BUT, BUT, BUT...

OPERA SEEMS SO...

INTIMIDATING!?

Let me give you some motherly advice: Treat Opera like a junkyard dog: If you're ever attacked by a rabid junkyard Opera, don't run, don't move, above all don't show fear. Just lie there and relax, dude.

It's just MUSIC! (Well, maybe not aaallll of it; 90% of it is music.)

(Unless it's German Opera; then 12 to 27% of it is music.)

That was a joke.
(Sort of.)

Let us start with the radical assumption that Opera is just plain music. Not snob music. Not uppity music. *Gettin down music.* Italian rock'n'roll, R&B, Gospel, let-it-all-hang-out music.

Italian **SOUL** music!

YOU PROBABLY THINK I'M MAKING THIS UP.

HA!

ITALIAN SOUL

"It's difficult to talk about soul without being misunderstood... A singer can have expression of soul, yet sing off pitch and out of rhythm and do nothing with the words. Expression of soul goes beyond the words into the realm of ineffable emotions. It used to be known as 'il fuoco sacro'—'the sacred fire.' Before that it was called 'Il cantar che nel'anima si sente '—singing that is sensed in the soul.'"

OPERA FANATIC Magazine [Spring, 1986] "Expressive Singing" by STEPHAN ZUCKER

7

Opera is **literally** Italian **SOUL** music!

It's no accident that Price, Norman, Battle & dozens of other black singers are starring in Opera houses all over the world. (I'll save my aria about the similarity between Opera & Gospel singing until later. It's about time for the Opera to hit the fan.)

First, a word about the organization of this book.

OPERA FOR **BEGINNERS** is divided into **4** easy pieces:

Opera History & Composers	Opera Singers

Listening to Opera: the Way It's **Really** Done	The Most Listener-Friendly Operas—& their Stories

WHY:
- ◆ To give you a clear and simple overview of Opera
- ◆ For quick & easy referencing—find what you want instantly
- ◆ To help you leap across entire chapters in a single bound—if your soul gets pushy.

(...reading about Opera is like reading about puberty:
—the words go one way, the feeling goes another.
If I were in your shoes [and I once was]
I would read ACT 3 (LISTENING TO OPERA) <u>first</u>.

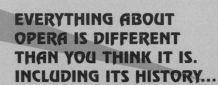

Be brave;
Listen to
the music.

WARNING

OPERA IS A LOT DIFFERENT THAN YOU THINK IT IS

I'M OUT TO GET YOU, BABY!

EVERYTHING ABOUT OPERA IS DIFFERENT THAN YOU THINK IT IS. INCLUDING ITS HISTORY...

ACT ONE:

Opera & HISTORY & COMPOSERS

"I DID _NOT_ SAY HISTORY
WAS BUNK.
I SAID IT WAS BUNK _TO ME_.
I DIDN'T NEED IT VERY BAD."
HENRY FORD

reOperatic R ts & early History

Opera's Ancient Roots
...or, Who do we BLAME?

Opera's origins are usually traced back to the Dramas of ancient Greece—and left at that—but that isn't playing fair with cultures that laid the groundwork and predated Greece by thousands of years. By the time Aeschylus wrote the first Greek "tragedy" (Drama), elegant dudes in Mesopotamia, Africa, and the Far East had been refining Music and Literature for 3000 years!

Here are a few of the highlights:

4000	BC	Harps & Flutes are being played in Egypt
3000	BC	The Egyptians invent the HEB-SED
		Sumerians [Iraq] write the first Epic Tale: *Gilgamesh*
2500	BC	Chinese develop a five-tone musical scale
		The first Epic Poetry is written in Babylonia [Iraq]
2000	BC	The first Novel is written in Egypt: *Story of Sinhue*
1000	BC	Professional musicians sing & play in ancient Israel
800	BC	Earliest written music appears in Sumeria [Iraq]
484	BC	Aeschylus FINALLY writes the first Greek Tragedy

By the time Uncle Aeschylus wrote the first Greek Drama, the Egyptians had been doing the HEB-SED for 2500 years!

"SKUZA, BRO', BUT...WHAT IS A 'HEB-SED?'"

The "HEB-SED"

In old, <u>old</u>, OLD Egypt, when the king got too rickety to rock'n'rule, they iced the old fart! Around 3000 BC, the Egyptians, creative dudes that they were, decided to try replacing the <u>real</u> murder with a ritual "pretend" murder: the Heb-sed.

> "IMAGINE THAT! YOU DON'T HAVE TO KILL PEOPLE ONSTAGE. YOU CAN GET THE EFFECT BY JUST <u>PRETENDING</u> TO!"

The Heb-sed evolved into Passion Plays, in which the Egyptians acted out stories from Egypt's glorious past. Evidence suggests that the Passion Plays were sung and accompanied by music.

Around 600 BC, hundreds of Greek ships hit the sea to escape the grouchy Spartans. So many Greeks settled in Egypt that the Pharaoh gave them a city! The Greeks were impressed with Egyptian temples, Egyptian religion and, baby, were they impressed with the Egyptian Passion Plays!

In 484 BC, Aeschylus wrote the first Greek "tragedy."

The Heb-sed—the root of Greek tragedy—was created by Egyptians—Africans, many of whom were <u>black</u>—some 2500 years before the Greeks "invented" Drama. It isn't a question of multiculturalism. It's a matter of intellectual honesty.

> ...SO THE GREEKS INVENTED DRAMA IN APPROXIMATELY THE SAME WAY THAT PAT BOONE INVENTED "BLUEBERRY HILL"—CAPISH?

If you're looking for someone to blame Opera on, blame the Egyptians—the black ones and tan ones—blame the Mesopotamians, blame the Chinese, blame the Greeks. And the Italians? Please, God, don't make me think about those damned Italians...

Maybe we could, like, vacation briefly in Ancient Greece?

11

The Ancient Geeks

(I mean Greeks)

Aristotle

From what historians know of Greek tragedy, much of the play was chanted or sung. Although the music hasn't survived, Aristotle and other ancient dudes declare that Music was an important part of Greek tragedy.

From Brother Aristotle's famous definition of tragedy:

Tragedy...is the imitation of some action that is important, entire...by language, ornamented & rendered pleasurable...

...in some parts meter alone is employed, in others, melody.

Music

The musical parts of Greek tragedy were never allowed to stand on their own or to compete with the text. Greek playwrights believed that the Music had to be kept within strict bounds or it would overpower the Drama.

IT'S NOT THAT THE GREEKS WERE AFRAID OF MUSIC—THEY JUST UNDERSTOOD ITS POWER.

Music

Greek playwrights didn't mix comedy and tragedy. Greek <u>comedy</u> was <u>spoken</u>— although the chorus was sung.

THE CHORUS WAS OFTEN IN THE FORM OF ANIMALS—FLIES, FROGS OR SHEEP—AND THEIR SINGING FOOLISHLY PARODIED THE CHANTING TRAGIC CHORUSES.

Roman dramas also used music. Roman actors and actresses sometimes sang their lines, as did the choruses. The tragedies of Seneca—plays like *Medea, The Trojans,* and *Hercules on Oeta*—followed the Greek model and included a chorus to be sung.

Some historians consider Roman comedies as the grandaddy of our Broadway musicals. The two most famous Roman comic playwrights, Plautus and Terence, used songs in their plays...

. . . then we spent the next thousand years waiting for something cool to happen.

Stephen Sondheim's *A Funny Thing Happened on the Way to the Forum* [1962], was a takeoff on Roman musical comedy.

The Dark Ages

The Middle Ages

"...zzz...ZZZ...ZZZ"

Would you rather die of:
A. The Plague
B. The Church
C. Boredom
D. All of the above

Limping Toward the Renaissance

Inspired by greed, power, and several utterly insane versions of Christianity, "the Church" killed Jews, Muslims, Christians, and free thinking of any kind. That lasted for several bloody centuries until the 14th century, when the rise of the great city-states of nortern Italy brought the brain-dead Middle Ages to a halt.

What little musicky drama existed during the Middle Ages revolved around religion. Priests and nuns mounted Easter and Christmas plays that, when combined with Gregorian chants, became what is called <u>pre</u>Operatic.

The "Quem Queritis" Plays

The most famous of the preOperatic church dramas is the *Quem Queritis* play (*Quem Queritis* means "Whom do you seek?"). In these Eastertime plays, a group of women go to the tomb to annoint Christ's body. At the tomb, an angel asks them whom they seek. When they say they seek Jesus, the angel tells them that Christ has risen from the dead. This brief encounter was staged and sung; other characters were added; eventually, it presented the whole story of Christ's crucifixion—all or mostly sung.

As these plays evolved they became more theatrical and less religious. They began to include figures like bawdy devils, which became so popular with the audience that the bishops ordered the plays removed from the church and into the village marketplaces.

Finally, after centuries of hibernation, people began to wake up.

They called their awakening "the Renaissance"—the rebirth.

To them, it was a return to ancient Greece...

The Renaissance

Italy

LOVE THE PEACE AND QUIET, HATE THE HAIRCUT...

Italy was the home of Michelangelo and Leonardo. Italy was the place where Vivaldi hid in a monastery in fake monkhood just so he could write a few hit tunes. Italy was the stomping-ground of princes and Popes. Italy was the place where rich dudes with time, money, and brains made grand plans to perfect man and beautify the world. No two ways about it: Italy was the heart, soul, and pocket-book of the Renaissance.

The Camerata Group

The Camerata Group, sponsored by Count Giovanni Bardi, was founded in Florence, Italy in 1580. The group—composed of scholars who were also poets, singers, musicians ("Renaissance men")—met regularly to rap about Greek culture. In no time, they came up with a nifty theory: If you combine serious drama with serious music, you enhance the power of both.

IF YOU THINK THAT SOUNDS A LITTLE LIKE GREEK TRAGEDY, YOU HIT THE WHALE RIGHT ON THE HEAD!

The Greeks "borrow" from the Egyptians, the Italians borrow from the Greeks (then Wagner takes credit for everything).

Count Bardi, on a roll, commissioned his Camerata dudes to produce a modern version of the ancient Greek art form.

BEAT IT KID. YOU'RE BOTHERIN' ME.

The First REAL Opera

In 1597 Jacopo Peri, with a libretto (words/story/text) by Ottavio Rinuccini, wrote Dafne (based on the Greek myth of the bimbo who turned into a tree). Dafne, the first "modern" Opera, was an instant success. The music has been lost, but from all accounts, the music was secondary to the play, a relationship that continued through the early years of Opera. To Opera's early masterminds, the story was far more important than the music.

The Earliest Surviving Opera

The earliest surviving Opera— also by Peri & Rinuccini—was

EURIDICE

composed in 1600.

The people went crazy for it. Quicker than you can say "Play it again, Sam," Opera spread from Florence to Rome, Venice and all the other major cities in Italy.

Everyone LOVED it!
(Well, not quite everyone . . .)

In 1697, Pope Innocent XI ordered an Opera house burned to the ground.

HE DIDN'T TELL ME WHY.

7

EARLY COMPOSERS 1600-1800

Monteverdi:

The People's Genius

Opera changed drastically once it moved to Venice and into the hands and heart of **Claudio Monteverdi** (1567-1643). Monteverdi wrote his first Opera, <u>Orfeo</u>, in 1607. The text (by **Striggio**) was similar to that of the old Camerata dudes but Monteverdi, an authentic genius, wrote real music. The old rascal even included a few dances!

The first public Opera house (San Cassiano) opened in Venice in 1637. There, Monteverdi could work for large groups of people instead of the few filthy-rich Greek wannabes in the Camerata Group. The large audience of "real" people made it clear that they didn't dig the talky version of Opera (called **arioso**):

- They wanted <u>music</u>—*even if it delayed the Opera's action.*
- They wanted <u>songs</u>—*even if they stopped the story dead!*
- They wanted <u>fancy</u> songs—*even if the words couldn't be understood!*

His audience was more important to Monteverdi than some sugar-daddy's academic theory, so he shifted the emphasis from dramatic action to more musical Opera. By 1670, there were public Opera houses in Florence, Rome, Genoa, Bologna, and Modena—and 20 in Venice—which, thanks to Mr. Monteverdi, had become the Opera capital of the world. Two of his Venetian Operas survive: <u>**Il Ritorno d'Ulisse**</u> (1641) and <u>**L'Incoronazione di Poppea**</u> (1642).

ARIA & RECITATIVO:
Opera Becomes a Singer's Art

Story—at least some semblance of it—was all that separated Opera from a list of Top Twenty tunes, so Monteverdi & Co. (his pupils) couldn't trash the story altogether. If the audience hated the talky *arioso* form, Opera's early geniuses would have to come up with something to replace it. So they did!

Monteverdi and the boys, acting with the wisdom of Solomon, divided the *arioso* into two parts: the **aria** & **recitativo**.

AN ARIA WAS A REAL SONG THAT WAS SUNG SOLO.

THE RECITATIVO TOLD THE STORY, OFTEN WITH ONLY HARPSICHORD ACCOMPANIMENT.

Opera was becoming a series of arias interrupted by just enough recitativo to tell the story. Opera now offered more vocal display and less serious drama. The audience loved it. What they wanted was some bodacious singing.

Enter "the **Castrati**," the *divos*. . .the first rock-'n'roll stars. But we'll save them for the section on singers. For now, let's get back to composers—and to the overall design of Opera itself.

Italy was, by a Texas mile, the birthplace of Opera—nobody disagrees with that—but you could make a pretty good case for England being second in importance during Opera's earliest days.

Since we're about to change countries, our point will be better made if we take a step backward in time as well:

The "MASQUES" and The MASTER

The Italian *mascherata*, the French *masquerade*, and the English *masque* were different names for a pre-Operatic form of "royal enter-tainment" that used poetry, dance, and music...but no Drama. They were called "masques" (God, I hate saying things like this) because the performers often wore...<u>masks</u>!

    Technically, the English masques had no Drama, so all of this would be forgettable if it weren't a great-souled British dude named **Henry Purcell** (1669-1695). Purcell wrote the music for many masques at the English court. The power and beauty of his best music is breathtaking.

What the hell—as long as we're in England . . .

HANDEL: Havin' It Both Ways

The pump don't work 'cause the vandals stole the handle.
BOB DYLAN

#☆ HANDEL ARIAS GET ME EVERY TIME...

George Frideric Handel (1685-1759) was born in Germany, studied music in Italy, then swam over to London (1710), where he became the most successful writer of Italian "Opera Seria" of his time. Handel wrote 35 Operas for London, each filled with the impossibly difficult coloratura arias that the castrati loved to show-off on...*and that the public loved.* Both **Rinaldo** (1711) and **Alcina** (1735) achieved great success with London audiences.

Haunted by Greek Tragedy

Handel wasn't satisfied with writing Operas that would showoff his Cadillac-without-an-engine singers. He also wrote Operas that sustained dramatic interest and featured characters that the audience could admire. In the words of critic Donald Grout:

Handel's dramatic creations are universal, ideal types of humanity... . If his characters suffer, the music gives full, eloquent expression to their sorrows... We are moved by the spectacle of suffering, but our compassion is mingled with...pride that we ourselves belong to a species capable of such heroism.

For a magnificent illustration of Handel's "nobly suffering characters," check out Jan Peerce singing the aria "Total eclipse" from <u>Sampson</u>.

21

Van Gogh's Other Ear

Whether Handel's Operas did or didn't achieve the stature of Greek tragedy (or Mexican tragedy), they were *fabulously* popular in 18th century London. He was a natural showman: He used every stage spectacle he could beg, borrow, build, or steal. His use of the orchestra was impressive. And he wrote the most dazzling bouquet of arias that anyone had ever heard, from the simple, austere and simply beautiful to the flashiest, show-offiest, most fiendishly difficult arias for singers of every voice.

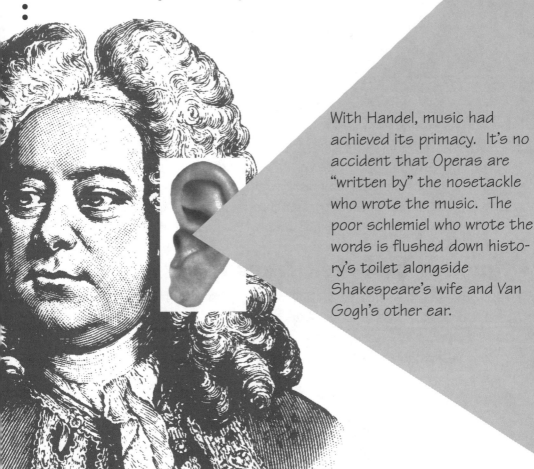

With Handel, music had achieved its primacy. It's no accident that Operas are "written by" the nosetackle who wrote the music. The poor schlemiel who wrote the words is flushed down history's toilet alongside Shakespeare's wife and Van Gogh's other ear.

Then along comes a vet blanket...

GLUCK: The First of Opera's Arty-Farty Reformers

AND CAN YOU IMAGINE WHO PERPETRATED THE FANCY SINGING? AN ARMY OF SINGING EUNUCHS!

By the mid-17th century, Vienna had become so cracked for Italian Opera that the Austrian royalty imported their own court composers, singers, and musicians. When they ran out of Italians, they settled for Germans. By the 18th century, the Viennese, like all of Europe, were grooving on the fact that Opera had become a true singers' art.

However: One of the imported Germans was an earnest cat named **Christoph Willibald Gluck** (1714-1787), referred to by Opera historians as a "reformer" (a word you'd normally use to describe prison wardens or saints on a mission from God). The no-nonsense Mr. Gluck seemed to be personally offended by the fact that the Italians had allowed Opera to degenerate into mere Music. Not even music! Singing! Fancy, schmancy singing.

Here We Go Again...

Commander Gluck wanted the poetry and drama of Opera to reflect the simplicity and power of Greek tragedy. He hated the hot-dog singers and their excessive vocal ornamentation. In his Operas **Orfeo ed Euridice** (1762) and **Alceste** (1767), Gluck tried to bring the quiet restraint of Greek drama into Viennese Opera.

Opera, from day one, had been a balancing act—or a war—between Drama and Music. As a rule, the Germans have lined up behind Drama and the Italians have formed a messy circle behind Music. Fortunately, there are exceptions to every rule . . .

MOZART: The Beloved Twerp

In music, one is always being asked, "Who is your favorite composer?" The safe answer... is to hedge and to say: certain works by certain composers.... But with Mozart, we my safely throw all caution to the winds: Mozart was the greatest composer who ever lived and who ever will live.

from WHO'S AFRAID OF CLASSICAL MUSIC by MICHAEL WALSH, music critic for TIME MAGAZINE!

Wolfgang Amadeus Mozart (1756-1791) was born in Salzburg, Austria on January 27. About eleven minutes later he was writing his own music. By age five he played the violin and the clavier (grandaddy of the piano); by age six, he could memorize a piece of music after one hearing—and he had already begun composing his own music. Mozart wrote his first Opera when he was 12 years old.

WHAT DID YOU BUY, EMPEROR JOJO?

BEE-GEES, CARPENTERS AND FRANKIE VALLI...

The Austrain emperor Josef II liked Mozart's music but loved the music of his court composer, Antonio Salieri.. (Musicologists consider that proof that Emperor JoJo was a tasteless bozo.)

AMADEUS

Although Salieri wrote dozens of Operas and was more successful than Mozart in his own time, the only thing Salieri is known for in *our* time is "poisoning" Mozart! If you haven't seen the movie *Amadeus*, scope it out. It's great fun and you get to hear some lifegiving music in little bite-size-chunks.

HOWEVER, SALIERI DID NOT POISON MOZART! THAT'S FICTION!

Singspiel

Although he died at 34, Mozart had an impact on three separate Operatic genres. One, the Singspiel, "singing play," is a German version of Broadway musical comedy, with spoken text and musical numbers.

MY FAVORITE MOZART OPERAS, THE ABDUCTION FROM THE SERAGLIO (1782) & THE MAGIC FLUTE (1791) ARE BOTH SINGSPIELS.

Opera SERIA

Mozart also wrote in the two most popular Opera forms of his day: Opera Seria (Serious) and Opera Buffa (Comic). <u>Idomeneo</u> (1781) & <u>La Clemenza di Tito</u> (1791) are Opera Seria. They're considered artificial by today's rules, but they contain nifty music.

Opera BUFFA— Mozart's Greatest Hits

The Operas generally considered Mozart's greatest, are his three comic Operas: <u>The Marriage of Figaro</u> (1786), <u>Don Giovanni</u> (1787), and <u>Cosi fan tutte</u> (1790). Some people consider Mozart the greatest composer of Operas in the 18th century (I'll dispute that later), but it would be only a slight exaggeration to say that the 18th century had been a mere Prologue.

Opera didn't become Opera until the Age of *Bel Canto*.

Scene 3:

Bel Canto =
"Beautiful Song" or
"Beautiful Singing"

The Bell Canto Complsers

3 Geniuses or 3 STOOGES?

In Opera, the early 19th century is known as the **Age of Bel Canto**. The three great Bel Canto composers—Rossini, Donizetti, and Bellini—developed a new kind of music that demanded a new art of singing. The singers responded by developing new singing techniques. At times, they even led the composers.

Making Opera Wall-to-Wall MUSIC

The Bel Canto composers continued the Italian tradition of giving Music, Melody, and Voice top billing in Opera. They helped liberate Opera from talk by eliminating much **recitativo secco**.

RECITATIVO SECCO = the stuff you hear in older Operas that sounds more like *talking* (recitativo) than singing, accompanied by a harpsichord (it sounds like a piano with mittens).

Instead of merely using the harpsichord in recitativo, Bellini and Donizetti used the full orchestra, turning even the "talk" into music. Rossini?

PLEASE, GOD, DON'T MAKE ME THINK ABOUT THAT MANIAC ROSSINI.

ROSSINI: The Lone Ranger Meets the Marx Brothers

Gioacchino Rossini (1792-1868) had the unique ability to write music that was *funny* and *brilliant* at the same time.

THE ONLY PERSON I CAN THINK OF WHO COULD WRITE MUSIC THAT WAS SIMULTANEOUSLY FUNNY & BRILLIANT IS THELONIUS MONK.

Rossini's comic Operas, full of melody, wit and genius, include **The Italian Girl in Algiers** (1813), **The Turk in Italy** (1814), **The Barber of Seville** (1816) & **Cinderella** (1817).

TWO VEEKS?

One of Opera's Favorite Legends: Rossini wrote **THE BARBER OF SEVILLE** (arguably the greatest comic Opera of all time?) in 2 weeks!

YEP. TWO STINKIN VEEKS!

GROUCHO's Serious Side

Rossini also wrote several very successful serious Operas, including **Tancredi** (1813), **Moses in Egypt** (1818), **Semiramide** (1823), **Otello** (1816), and **William Tell** (1829).

Rossini's comic Operas are still popular but his serious Operas are staged less often nowadays. Why? Maybe the 18th century Opera Seria form is out of fashion. Maybe its flashy singing roles and general artificiality strike modern critics as dramatically unconvincing.

OR MAYBE WE AREN'T AS SMART AS WE THINK WE ARE?

Legends, WiseCracks & Disagreements

WELL, ROSSINI, DON'T QUIT YOUR DAY JOB...

LEGENDARY MEETINGS: Rossini dropped by Beethoven's cave to pay his respects to the deaf old godfather of symphony. Beethoven, who had written one dead-serious Opera and was as grouchy as he looked, told Rossini to stick to comic Operas.

Legendary Remarks: Rossini once said, "Too bad I wasn't born German; I might have made something of myself." In every case the quoter took Rossini's words as an admission that his critics were right—he <u>was</u> as lazy as he was talented and wasted his gifts.

TOO BAD I WASN'T BORN A CRITIC, I MIGHT HAVE MADE SOMETHING OF MYSELF.

I Disagree: Rossini was one the great smartasses of all time. There are entire books devoted to his wisecracks. I think he was bustin our chops. I think it's so obvious that only a humor-impaired, German-minded critic could miss it.

Groucho's OTHER Serious Side

EVEN IF YOU CAN'T UNDERSTAND A WORD, THEY'RE FUNNY.

Another of Rossini's contributions to Opera was his use of voices in combination. The ensembles that end nearly every act of his comic Operas are unmatched for sheer vitality.

And Rossini's much maligned crescendoes—pure energy! If you can sit still during a Rossini overture, you better check your pulse (that reminds me of a joke, but it's a little bit sexist, so I'll skip it), she's—you're—probably dead.

From Sublime to Ridiculous

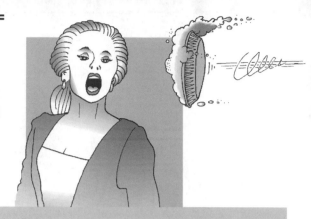

Mr. Rossini had about twelve different kinds of sublime and about 150 kinds of ridiculous.

Sublime:

- Desdemona's long aria at the end of Rossini's <u>Otello</u>—especially as sung by Frederika von Stade.
- The duets in <u>Semiramide</u>, sung with outrageous flair by Joan Sutherland and Marilyn Horne.
- The rondo in <u>Moses.</u>
- Any Rossini aria sung by Cecilia Bartoli.

Riduculous:

- The end of every Act in <u>The Barber of Seville</u>—especially the whacked out "Fredda immobile" ("Frozen with fright") bit!
- The "Pappatacci" ("eat and shut up") ensemble from <u>The Italian Girl in Algiers</u> is probably the most ridiculous piece of music ever!

Simultaneously *Sublime* and Riduculous:

- Ugo Benelli singing Rossini's <u>Messa de Gloria</u>—technically not an Opera—it's a Mass, but it's probably the only funny Mass God ever had written to Him!

Rossini is one of those guys, like Thelonious Monk, you wish they'd done an autopsy on. They must have been Martians...or something. No mere human being could have been as profoundly off the wall as those guys were.

ROSSINI, LOVE YOU BRO— THANKS FOR ALL THAT GOOD CHIT YOU LEFT US.

I ♥ ROSSINI

DONIZETTI: Mad Scenes & English Queens

Gaetano Donizetti (1797-1848), son of a pawnshop caretaker and a seamstress, added a dramatic urgency to Bel Canto Opera that foreshadowed Verdi and *verismo*. Donizetti incorporated drama into Opera with greater realism than any composer of his time. While Rossini used 18th century plots about heroes descended from pottery (or was that *poetry?*) Donizetti used the realistic theater of the early 19th Century. As a result, many of his Operas are frequently performed, especially **Lucia de Lammermoor** (1835). His Operas **Anna Bolena** (1830), **Maria Stuarda** (1834), and **Roberto Devereux** (1837), loosely based on English history, are vocal and dramatic challenges, especially for the leading soprano.

> One of the most moving, beautiful, performances of Opera in English is Janet Baker singing Donizetti's **Maria Stuarda**.

Donizetti's comedies are still performed: **The Elixir of Love** (1832) has been a showcase for every great tenor from Caruso to Pavarotti. And speaking of Pavarotti...

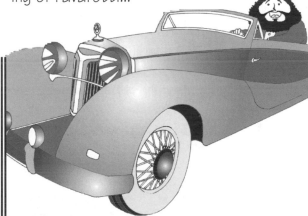

Donizetti's **Daughter of the Regiment** (1840) was the Opera in which Big Luch hit super-stardom—thanks largely to the aria in which the beautiful singing fat guy hit nine high Cs. Between Luchiano and Joan Sutherland, you had a 500lb nightingale "flying" around the stage.

His Final Mad Scene

Maybe it's just a coincidence, but Donizetti, the composer of Opera's most famous Mad Scene (in **Lucia de Lammermoor**), went mad and spent the last years of his life in an insane asylum.

BELLINI: If Hamlet Had Written an Opera...

Vincenzo Bellini (1801-1835) was a perfect romantic nitwit—the kind of space cadet you'd expect to write poems in a locked diary and die of unrequited love. Bellini wrote only ten Operas before he bit the dust at the age of 34, but they contained some of the most purely beautiful music ever written.

His Opera **Norma** became wildly popular when it was first staged in Milan in 1831 and is still going strong. One reason for Norma's success is its soprano-eatin' title role, which attracts risk takers of all kinds. It's one of the most difficult roles ever written for soprano. It demands tremendous breath control because of Bellini's long vocal line. Despite the fact that there are many fine recordings of Norma, it's one of those roles that is virtually "owned" by one person—in this case, Maria Callas.

BELLINI'S OTHER OPERAS, ESPECIALLY _LA SOMNAMBULA_ (1831) AND _I PURITANI_ (1835) ARE STILL STAGED WHENEVER SUPERHUMAN SINGERS ARE AVAILABLE.

Maria Callas' *"Qui la voce suoa suave..."* is one of the most moving arias ever recorded. (Toward the end of the aria is a fast section called the "cabaletta," which is part of most Bel Canto arias; I dislike it in most songs, and I hate it in this one. See what you think.

If there is any five minutes of singer-and-song that, to me, embodies the outrageous beauty of Bel Canto, it is the duet from La Somnambula, sung by Pavarotti and Sutherland... especially the moment when Pavarotti goes

"...SE MISERO,..."

...DON'T LOOK SO SURPRISED! DON'T PLAY DUMB WITH ME! YOU KNOW AS WELL AS I DO THAT BEL CANTO WAS SIMPLY TOO DAMNED BEAUTIFUL TO LAST...!

VERDI... LIKE CHARLIE THE TUNA

Giuseppi Verdi (1813-1901), arguably Italy's (or the *world's?*) greatest Opera composer, was, from his name to his music, a meat-&-potatoes guy. His name in English comes out roughly "Joe Green" and his music, at least in the beginning, was as subtle as a linebacker's hat. (The Italians called him "Verdi *bruto.*")

Verdi began by working in the Bel Canto style, but it was too pretty for him. Before long he began to develop his own style—a style simpler and more direct than the dazzle of Bel Canto. Verdi wrote over 25 Operas during his 50-year career. His work is usually divided into three periods.

"His thoughts, few that they were, lay silent in the privacy of his head."
—SPIKE MILLIGAN, *Puckoon*

The EARLY Period

His earliest works—<u>Nabucco</u> (1842), <u>I Lombardi</u> (1843), and <u>Ernani</u> (1844) combine the rhythm and energy of Rossini with the intense drama of Donizetti and the melodic genius of Bellini.

If you can find the quartet from <u>I Lombardi</u>, with Gigli, Pinza, Rethberg, & Tibbett, honey, your mind is liable to fall clean off! It has everything Opera has to offer, including the spiritual phoniness of the great Benjamno Gigli!

The MIDDLE Period

Verdi's middle Operas combined the dramatic intensity of his early period with more subtle orchestration and variations on the old Bel Canto forms. The masterpieces of the middle period include <u>Macbeth</u> (1847), <u>Rigoletto</u> (1851), <u>Il Trovatore</u> (1853), <u>La Traviata</u> (1853), and <u>La forza del destino</u> (1862). Unfortunately, even in his middle period, Verdi went weak in the knees for curses and coincidences and all the other melodramatic baloney that 19th century theater was full of. The two final Operas of Verdi's middle period are <u>Don Carlos</u> (1867) and <u>Aida</u> (1874).

CHARLEY the TUNA

Near the end of his career, when he was a <u>very</u> old man, Verdi wrote two Operas—<u>Otello</u> (1887) and <u>Falstaff</u> (1893). Most critics consider <u>Otello</u> and <u>Falstaff</u> Verdi's greatest Operas. Most normal people consider <u>Otello</u> and (especially) <u>Falstaff</u> Verdi's most boring Operas.

Verdi was like that old TV commercial about Charley the Tuna:

IF YOU WANTED OPERA THAT TASTED GOOD, YOU WENT TO VERDI AND THE ITALIANS.
IF YOU WANTED OPERA WITH GOOD TASTE, YOU VENT WITH WAGNER AND THE VUNDERBAR GERMANS...

The famous conductor Arturo Toscanini was sitting in on a rehearsal of Wagner's <u>Tristan und Isolde</u>. During the lonnnnnng love duet in Act Two, Toscanini turned to the woman next to him and said,

"IF THEY WERE ITALIANS, THEY WOULD ALREADY HAVE HAD SEVEN CHILDREN."

Scene 5:

RICHARD WAGNER

● **GENIUS OF MUSIC-DRAMA?**

● **Boring Megalomaniac?**

B●O●T●H?

BACKGROUND: Mr. Beethoven & Mr. Weber

In 1805, the smily Mr. Beethoven wrote his only Opera, **<u>Fidelio,</u>** which inspired a dude named Carl Maria von Weber to write <u>German</u> Operas—**<u>Der Freischutz</u>** (1824) & **<u>Oberon</u>** (1826)—based on <u>German</u> fairy tales, <u>German</u> folk music and, above all, <u>German</u> theories. (They weren't exactly racists, they just thought they were better than everyone else.)

That's where Wagner comes in . . .

Der BLUES BROTHERS

Richard Wagner (1813-1883) was born the same year as Verdi (but in a different century). Wagner *loved* theories.

> HE MUST'VE WONDERED HOW THE WEIRD ITALIANS COULD WRITE AN OPERA WITHOUT A THEORY BEHIND IT?

In 1849 Wagner wrote *The ArtVork of the Future.*

In 1851 he wrote *Opera & Drama.*

Wagner vent forth preaching the gospel of Music Drama.

I imagine Weber & Wagner as John Belushi and Dan Ackroyd in <u>The Blues Brothers</u>:

> "HI, THERE. WE'RE ON A MISSION FROM GOD."

COSIMA Liszt/von Bulow/Wagner/Lugosi

You may have heard stories claiming that Wagner was an arrogant, antiSemitic windbag. They're all true. And then some. He sponged off of a guy named Hans von Bulow, then stole his wife, Cosima (the daughter of the composer/pianist/stud Franz Liszt). Wagner and Cosima got it on while still living in the supernaturally passive von Bulow's house.

> REMARKABLY ENOUGH, WAGNER FOUND TIME TO WRITE AN OPERA OR TWO.

In 1843 he wrote **The Flying Dutchman**. In 1845 he wrote **Tannhauser.** In 1850, **Lohengrin**. In 1865, **Tristan und Isolde**. In 1868, **Die Meistersinger von Nurnberg**. In 1882, **Parsifal**. But it was the **Ring** cycle that gave him his rep.

That and Cosima Liszt/von Bulow/Wagner. There are two things in life I can't imagine: getting tackled by Lawrence Taylor and having sex with Cosima Wagner. No matter how they try to spruce her up, the woman sounds like something out of a Bela Lugosi movie ... dragging her foot, eating insects:

> "YOU RAAANG, MASTER?"

The RING OF THE NIBELUNGS

In 1848, Wagner began the Ring cycle of four Operas (Music-Dramas),

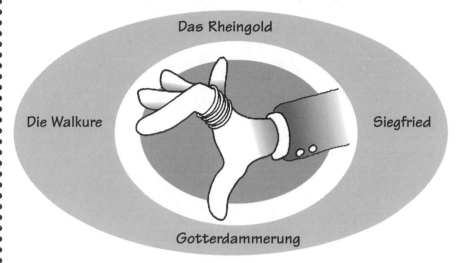

Das Rheingold

Die Walkure

Siegfried

Gotterdammerung

which premiered in Bayreuth* in 1876.

*BAYREUTH

There was no Opera house in the world excellent enough to perform his Ring cycle (or big enough to hold his ego), so Wagner conned King Ludwig (of Bavaria) into building one especially for him in Bayreuth. To "Wagnerians," Bayreuth is a holy place where, every year, they make the pilgrimage to see, hear, and experience hours of Little Richard's Operas.

(...I've never heard anybody admit this, but when I first read about Bayreuth, I thought: "Geeze, I didn't know they had Opera in Lebanon!" It isn't in Lebanon, it's in Germany; and you don't say BayROOT—you say BUYroit.)

How GOOD is Wagner?

★ **J.L. DeGaetani** (critic): "The Ring cycle is the greatest achievement in the history of Opera."

★ **G.B. Shaw** (playwright): championed Wagner for years. Then Shaw changed his mind with a vengeance! Ditto for Nietzsche!

★ **Rossini:** "Wagner has good moments but bad quarter-hours."

BOTTOM LINE

Wagner was one of the greatest composers and worst human beings of all time. Let's give Russian composer Mily Balakirev the last word...

"AFTER _LOHENGRIN_, I HAD A SPLITING HEADACHE AND ALL THROUGH THE NIGHT I DREAMED ABOUT A GOOSE."

Scene 6:

FRENCH DUDES

...Forced to Depend on the Talent of Strangers

By the beginning of the 19th century, Opera was the most popular entertainment in Europe and Paris had become its center. There was, however, a teensy weensy problem: The French, who were so gifted in painting, poetry and porn, couldn't seem to get the hang of writing Operas, so they imported Italians like Giovanni Battista Lulli and advertised them/him as the "French composer, **Jean-Baptiste Lully**."

At the end of the 18th century, the extremely Italian **Luigi Cherubini** (1760-1842) settled in Paris and wrote several successful Operas, most notably <u>Medea</u> (1797), a magnificent Opera we might never have heard if it weren't for mighty Maria Callas. (See chapter on Singers.)

French GRAND Opera

When the French finally did get the hang of writing Opera, critics everywhere moaned. The hodge-podge they created, known as "French Grand Opera," was a cross between Barnum & Bailey, talky Opera and ballet.

Lully is usually "credited" with starting French grand Opera, but it was **Giacomo Meyerbeer** who "perfected" it in <u>**Les Huguenots**</u> (1836) and <u>**Le Prophete**</u> (1849).

    Charles Gounod (1818-1893) wrote the extremely popular Opera <u>**Faust**</u> (1859), and the slightly less popular <u>**Romeo et Juliet**</u> (1867)— which, as one bitchy critic put it, "suffers from the musical tastes of the day."

BALLET?

YES, BALLET!

Laugh & Cry

Jacques Offenbach (1819-1880), the enormously successful writer of witty, irreverent operettas, took a shot at respectability (and hit *immortality!*) by writing one fairly serious Opera —<u>**The Tales of Hoffmann**</u> (1880).

Jules Massenet (1842-1912) composed several sentimental but extremely listenable Operas. At least two of them — <u>**Manon**</u> (1884) and <u>**Werther**</u> (1892) are still performed today.

BERLIOZ: the Godfather of SNOB

Hector Berlioz was the first in a line of French composers whose music was not so much *written* as it was *orchestrated*. Like Wagner and his army of musical Germans, Berlioz was on a mission from God to stomp out the Italians who were undermining the world by filling it with beautiful music. Here is Berlioz hizzelf:

On arriving in Milan, out of a sense of duty, I made myself go to hear the latest opera [Donizetti's L'elisir d'amore].

I found the theater full of people talking in normal voices, with their backs to the stage. The singers, undeterred...yelled their lungs out in the strictest spirit of rivalry.... People were gambling, eating supper in their boxes, etcetera....

Music for the Italians is a sensual pleasure and nothing more.... They want a score that, like a plate of macaroni, can be assimilated immediately without their having to think about it...

From the snooty **MEMOIRS** of HECTOR BERLIOZ

Dear Mr. Berlioz: In the words of that Old Italian Master, Yogi Berra:

"You can't think and hit at the same time."

CONFESSION:

In Opera (as in Rock, R&B, or Jazz), <u>my</u> *likes* or *dislikes* have as much or more to do with the singer than with the song—or Opera. As far as I'm concerned, Berlioz is a real snorer.

<u>HOWEVER</u>: if you get Jessye Norman and Placido Flamingo, both at the peak of their glory, singing <u>Les Troyens</u> (1858), suddenly Berlioz' foppish music becomes supercharged, dramatic, thrilling. But, hey: Norman and Domingo in peak voice could sing the Ingredients off a cereal box and it'd sound supercharged, dramatic, thrilling.

The seven French composers I've mentioned don't add up to Verdi's shoe or Wagner's hat. Oddly enough, France's greatest contribution to Opera was not Operatic—it was literary.

NOT A CHANCE.

I'LL TRADE YOU ALL MY FRENCH COMPOSERS FOR ONE OF YOUR VERDI'S.

45

"VERISMO": True-to-Life Opera

(...or, Anything that happens in Sicily...)

YOU MEAN LIKE GYPSIES!

The French, like the Americans, periodically show great concern for poor and victimized people. And, like the Americans, they seldom do anything practical for them; instead, they paint pictures of them. Or "study" them like bugs in a jar. Or write books about them: Toward the end of the 19th century, French novelists like Zola and Merimee created a new literary style referred to as "realism" or "naturalism." Offhand you might think that a realistic novel would be about normal, average people. Ha! Naturalistic novels—and the Operas that resembled them—were full of murder, revenge, rage—they were usually about "the underbelly of society."

The MOST FAMOUS French Opera

In 1874, after a mediocre start as a composer, **George Bizet** (1838-1875) wrote

CARMEN

the most famous of all French Operas, and the first "naturalistic" Opera.

A few decent naturalistic French Operas followed (e.g. **Charpentier's** <u>Louise</u> (1900)...but it wasn't the French whose creative fires were ignited by naturalism...

CAV & PAG

Realism ("Verismo") Italian Style

If there is any single Opera that *defines* Opera to most "normal" people, it is almost certainly **I Pagliacci**. If you decide to open your mind (& wallet) enough to actually <u>go</u> to the Opera house to <u>see</u> I Pagliacci, what you'll almost certainly find is a double-header referred to by Opera-dudes as **Cav** & **Pag**.

Cav is **Cavalleria Rusticana**, an Opera that, like I Pagliacci (as Yogi Berra would say), is so famous that nobody goes to see it anymore.

 **Petro Mascagni** (1863-1945) studied at the Milan (Italy) Conservatory under the famous composer Ponchelli.

Mascagni was a free spirit who hated all that discipline, so he left the Conservatory to join a touring Opera company.

In 1890, at the age of 27, he won first prize in a contest sponsored by the music publisher Sanzogno with his One Act Opera, **Cavalleria Rusticana**, based on a famous Sicilian tale by Giovanni Verga, featuring a jilted lover, dishonor, revenge and lots and lots of blood. "Stark, naked passion, expressed in unabashed violence" is how one book puts it.

NO WONDER IT WAS A GREAT SUCCESS!

Almost overnight, <u>Cav</u> was in demand all over the world, with premieres at Opera houses all over Italy, plus Moscow, Vienna, Madrid, Stockholm, you name it, while Opera houses in New York had bidding wars for the rights to the first US performance.

> I MORTGAGED THE HOUSE AND SOLD THE CAR, BUT WE'RE GONNA SEE CAV.

PAG Ruggiero Leoncavallo (1858-1919), an ambitious Neapolitan (from Naples, not three-colored) composer who had been working hard without much luck, struck it rich in 1892, with his Opera **I Pagliacc**i, a story where Caruso catches a baritone sneaking around with his wife, so he kills both of them in an outpouring of blood, tears and melody.

> VERISMO: BLOOD, GUTS AND MELODY.

> (OR ANY OPERA THAT TAKES PLACE IN SICILY.)

Both Leoncavallo and Mascagni wrote other Operas but to the Opera world, they're one-shot-Charlies—<u>Cav</u> & <u>Pag</u>.

Russian & Slavic Opera

The Italians went into Russia and Eastern Europe, as they'd gone everywhere else,

playing, writing, singing and teaching Opera to anyone who'd listen. In Russia and Eastern Europe the Italians met the same fate they'd met everywhere else: They were welcomed at first as bearers of precious gifts, then resented by the "natives," who set out on a mission to de-Italianize Opera, to nationalize it with their own country's myths and melodies.

After a mere 150 years of Italian coaching, the Russians began writing their own Operas. And they were good ones. **Glinka**, **Borodin** and **Rimsky-Korsakov** wrote good Operas. Tchaikovsky's <u>Eugene Onegin</u> (1879) is better than good and Mussorgsky's <u>Boris Godunov</u> (1874) can be damn near a religious experience if you get the right singer for the title role.

20TH CENTURY OPERA

When choosing between two evils, I always like to take the one I've never tried before.

MAE WEST

Two 20th century composers—one Italian, one German—have dominated all others: Puccini & Strauss.

PUCCINI: Rapture of the Shallow

Giacomo Puccini (1858-1924) gets a load of badmouth from critics, but three of his Operas are among the most popular in the world.

La Boheme	1896
Tosca	1900
Madama Butterfly	1904

And several others aren't far behind...

Manon Lescault	1896
Fanciulla del West	1910
Trittico	1918
Turandot	1926

The Stephen Speilberg of Opera...?

Puccini combined the Italian musicality of Verdi, a smattering of the reforms of Wagner, and a great nose for what the public wanted. He was flashy but superficial—but maybe it didn't matter because the surface was so good; he liked women and he wasn't overly encumbered by artistic principles.

Puccini drove a big orchestra and wrote a hell of a tune. I mean a _hell of a tune_. He's the kind of guy you like better if you don't look too deep. Above all, observe The Two Don'ts: Don't ask yourself why the women in his Operas kept dying for love?

And don't ask yourself how someone that shallow can write tunes that move you to tears?

STRAUSS: Genius Without Soul...?

When it came to writing Operas, Richard Strauss (1864-1949) was a little bit all over the place: He wrote both mythic and realistic Operas, both tragic and comic Operas, and both discordant screechers and melodious hit-paraders.

   He started out as a musical radical, with a pair of dissonant, mythic hair-raisers: **Salome** (1905) and **Elektra** (1909)...

Salome ends the Opera named for her with a magnificent, raving, goose-bump-inducing several minute lust-filled nervous breakdown sung to John the Baptist's severed head!

And if that doesn't get your attention, Ducky, Maria Ewing (they aint all fat ladies!) did Salome's Dance of the Seven Veils with such total commitment to realism that she wound up buck nekked! I didn't see it but I read the reviews: they all sounded like they were written by guys who swear they buy Playboy for the articles.

SMACK!

Then Mr. Strauss mellowed out with <u>Der Rosenkavalier</u> (1911) and <u>Adriadne auf Naxos</u> (1912), two *nice* Operas with tunes you can hum (if you're Jessye Norman).

HUGO von Hofmannsthal

With <u>Elektra,</u> Strauss began a long collaboration with the poet Hugo von Hofmannsthal, one of the greatest librettists (the dude who writes the words) ever. In July 1929, Hofmannsthal's son committed suicide; the poet died of a heart-attack on the way to the funeral.

Genius-Without-Soul Brothers?

Strauss was often accused of being "a Genius Without Soul." Why? He was too good at too many things. He did everything well, but there was no sense of compulsion. A genius who is uncompelled is merely a very smart guy. He wrote music sort of like he was experimenting with rats.

The "Genius Without Soul" tag is part of the usual critical rap about Strauss, so you can say it without being rubberhosed by the Music Correctness Police. But what I'm about to say is sure to put me on the hit list of every music critic in town: In my opinion, Mozart was also a genius without soul. To be fair, I do think that occasionally a little soul did sneak into Mozart's music.

BUT TO ME HE WAS 90% GLIB/FACILE/TALENT AND 10% SOUL.
TO <u>ME</u>, MOST OF HIS MUSIC SOUNDS LIKE IT WAS WRITTEN BY A PRISSY LITTLE PRIG IN A POWDERED WIG; TO ME, MOZART IS THE MOST OVERRATED COMPOSER OF OPERA AROUND.

I don't expect any love letters from the goons who guard the gates of the Mausoleum of Musical Theology, but for those of you who are new to classical music—or who like to make up your own minds without being conned or coerced—here are a few facts:

AHH, MR. BOLTON... YOU'LL BE STAYING IN THE "MOZART SUITE"...

WELCOME TO HEAVEN

☞ Much of Mozart's fame rested on his accomplishments as a *child prodigy.* His contemporaries were less impressed by the grown man.

☞ During his lifetime, Mozart was nowhere near as successful as Salieri—and several other guys you've never heard of.

☞ Mozart was pretty much ignored until the mid 20th century. He was canonized 50-100 years ago.

☞ American critics and academics—it's the fashion of the day—are currently in love with German music.

Maybe you think I'm exaggerating. America's all-purpose smart-ass, H.L. Mencken wrote:

> "There are only two kinds of music; German music and bad music."

From the preface of *The Opera Omnibus,* by Irving Kolodin:
> "The name [Caruso] clearly gave warning of an Italian, thus of a person not to be trusted with 'higher musical values.'"

In fairness to Kolodin, he was poking fun at the pro-German/ anti-Italian bias he had started with. He didn't realize that he never got rid of it.

The worst part of the pro-German bias isn't the way it bullies listeners, it's the invisible straight-jacket it puts on singers...

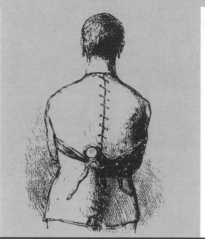

"Today's singer is appallingly restricted whether he knows it or not. From his earliest student days he is subjected to a kind of musical guidance grounded in a Germanic philosophy of the sanctity of composition and the immutablility of the written note.... From the beginning to the end of his career the singer's every utterance is supervised by that 'police escort' which the virtuosos of the end of the 18th century discerned in Mozart's orchestral accompaniments. "

HENRY PLEASANTS—*THE GREAT SINGERS*

It wasn't always that way. In the formative days, singers shaped Opera right alongside the composers...

WHETHER THE COMPOSERS LIKED IT OR NOT!

The legendary contralto Marian Anderson tried for months to meet Sol Hurok (the Don King of 1930s music), but Hurok was a busy guy. One day he dropped by a concert she was singing in Paris. Years later Hurok admitted how he felt when he first heard Marian Anderson's voice:

"Chills danced up my spine and my palms were wet."

ACT TWO:

Opera singers say that singing a high note is a very sexy experience. I've never sung one so I can't say. What I can say is that being in the same room with someone who sings one is shocking. You don't hear it as much as you feel it.

I've never been in a room with a singer anywhere near the quality of Marian Anderson, but let me tell you, many of the better amateur Opera singers I know can make you feel things in places you never knew you had. Is it "sexy?" Sexy pretty much refers to what happens in one little X-rated neighborhood of your body. A highnote happens—or seems to happen—to every cell of you. Your toes curl, your armpits warm, and you feel sexy and spiritual and very much alive...

Opera SINGERS

The Operatic Voice

CITIUS, ALTIUS, FORTIUS
(SWIFTER, HIGHER, STRONGER)
Motto of the Olympic
Games

Despite the arrogant Diva bit, most Opera singers are not only humble about their voices, they're scared witless of them. Singers generally say <u>the </u>voice, not <u>my</u> voice, as if the voice was something that didn't belong to them, something as arbitrary and moody as the Ocean.

The Voice, like love, is a *gift*: No matter how pretty or worthy or cool you are, you can't *earn* it, you don't *deserve* it, and it's liable to run off with the next good-looking stranger who comes along.

Mahalia Jackson put it this way: "This is not *my* voice. This is God's Voice. He sings through me. And when He is finished with me, He will sing through someone else."

If you have a fair-to-middlin' voice, you may have some control...

BUT WHO CARES?

If you have *The Voice*, you don't control it, it controls you...so you try to appease it by driving yourself crazy with lack of sex (DelMonaco) or you prowl around backstage like a nitwit looking for bent nails (Pavarotti).

58

Opera as an Olympic Sport

No self-respecting Opera critic could say this but, tacky dude that I am, I am free to admit that one of the attractions of Opera is that Opera singers can sing <u>higher</u> than anyone else. And <u>lower</u>. Not to mention, <u>softer</u>, <u>louder</u>, <u>faster</u>, <u>slower</u>. They can hold notes longer. They can do trills and crescendoes and diminuendos and other phenomenally fancy tricks that "normal" singers couldn't dream of. These people are the Michael Jordans and Jackie Joyner Kersees and Joe Montanas of singing.

> PERSONALLY, I WISH THEY'D MAKE OPERA SINGING AN OLYMPIC SPORT.

The Opera Voice—
A Few Basics

Opera singers are divided into categories, depending primarily on their "range" (how high or low they can sing):

Women are either Sopranos (high), Mezzos (medium), or Contraltos (low).

Men are Tenors (high), Baritones (medium), Basses (low).

Each category is divided into subcategories, depending on the Range, Size (volume or loudness), Agility (ability to sing fast, fancy stuff), Color (hard to define things like the brightness or youthfulness or warmth of a voice), and, oddly enough, Emotional Disposition.

Voice Teachers may be the weirdest people in the world: I knew one who—I swear to God—divided women into voice categories by the size of their boobs. If you had cute little lemonade squeezers, you were a Coloratura; if you had a pair of watermelons, you were a Mezzo.

I LEFT THE ROOM BEFORE HE STARTED DEMONSTRATING HIS TECHNIQUE FOR SEPARATING TENORS FROM BASSES.

The Categories & Subdivisions

Sopranos

Coloratura: very high, very agile,
Lyric: what most people would consider a *beautiful* voice
Spinto: a lyric soprano with more size and intensity
Dramatic: a big, loud, emotionally intense voice
   ...or a combination of the above—e.g., Maria Callas was a Dramatic Coloratura

Mezzo Sopranos

Lyric
Dramatic
   Coloratura, instead of being a separate category, is an add-on: e.g., Marilyn Horne is a Dramatic Coloratura Mezzo, but Cecilia Bartoli is a Lyric Coloratura Mezzo
Contralto: a very deep woman's voice (e.g., Marian Anderson's low range)

Tenor

Lyric: the most beautiful high male voice—often "small"
Spinto: a Lyric tenor with a larger, more intense voice
Dramatic: a large, strong, loud, asskicking male voice
Heldentenor: ("Heroic tenor") a VERY loud male voice that can be heard over the huge ego—I mean orchestra—in "Wagnerian" Opera
There is also a VERY high, VERY light voiced tenor, usually called a *Tenorino* or a "Rossini tenor;"
   Coloratura, as with Mezzos, is an add-on category—*except for the Rossini tenorino*—who must have it

Baritone

can be divided into Lyric/Spinto/Dramatic but more often:
Lyric Baritone:
Verdi Baritone:
Bass-Baritone:

Basso

Basso Cantante: e.g., Kurt Moll in Mozart's *Abduction from the Seraglio*
Basso Profundo: a deep, dark, sometime villainous, tone

THERE IS ALSO A CRITTER CALLED THE COUNTER TENOR. THE COUNTER TENOR IS THE CLOSEST THING WE HAVE TO...

"THE USUAL PROCEDURE
...[ALLEDGEDLY PAINLESS] WAS TO SOAK
THE BOY IN A VERY WARM BATH, PRESS
ON HIS JUGLAR VEIN UNTIL HE FAINTED
AND THEN CUT OFF THE FAMILY JEWELS."

...THE CASTRATI

Somewhere around the beginning of the Renaissance, the Pope and all the other holy guys in Rome decided that women didn't belong in the church choirs. (Does anyone else get the feeling that the Big Three Monotheisms get nervous around women and sexuality or is it just me?) Anyhow, the holy guys with the pointed hats noticed that church choirs without the high, beautiful voices of women sounded low and dull and stayed in the church instead of reaching up to God.

Talk about a dilemma! No normal person could have solved that problem but the Pope is a privileged man who raps with God. Whether God told him or the Pope figured it out solo, the Popester came up with an ingenious but sick solution:

I DON'T BELIEVE IN COINCIDENCES.

The first "officially recognized" castrati (two of them) turned up in the Papal Choir in 1599; the first Opera was written in 1600.

Although the first Operas were talky imitations of Ancient Greek Tragedy, when Manelli's (1595-1667) *fairly musical* <u>Andromeda</u> opened at the Teatro San Cassiano in Venice in 1637, it touched off a flame that spread thorough Italy. The people didn't give a damn about a "theory" of Opera—***they wanted MUSIC!***

Opera, following Darwin's law of Survival of the Flashiest, evolved toward the much more musical Opera Seria.

The Big Three Venetians who transformed Opera from a talky impersonation of Ancient Greece to a true singer's art were **Monteverdi, Cavalli** (1602-1676), and **Cesti** (1620-1669).

"You maka me feeeeeel..."

At the time Mr. Manelli wrote his toe-tappin' Opera <u>Andromeda</u>, women, as we know, were forbidden to appear onstage in Rome, and "strongly discouraged" elsewhere in Italy—like Venice. So naturally, the choir of St. Mark's (Venice) was "manned" largely by Castrati, the geld-ed gentlemen who could sing as high as any ("You maka me feeeel...") natural woman.

So, ironic as it might seem to you Pagans, the same Catholic Church that presently excommunicates men who love other men, cre-ated a situation in which men were forced to sing songs dripping with passionate romantic love...*to other men!*

Why? Is there some deep, dark Freudian meaning in there?

Who knows? Maybe the Italians just dig high notes.

The Italians were so obsessed with high voices that even after they stopped using Castrati, they seemed to feel that the person with the highest voice should sing the principal role. So they stopped putting Castrati in heroic male roles—and replaced them with <u>women</u>! The result: **"Trouser Roles."**

PORGY AND BRUCE?

63

Trouser Roles

The practice of writing men's roles for women survived well into the 19th and 20th centuries, in Operas like Rossini's **Tancredi** and **Semiramide** (roles that helped make Marilyn Horne famous), **Tales of Hoffmann**, and **Rosenkavalier**.

Trouser Roles = roles written for women—usually mezzos or contraltos—to sing the parts of men.

Even the Italians, despite their well-advertised libidos, just couldn't seem to get that gender business straight. I'm no homophobe (some of my best friends are straight), but when Bellini turned Romeo into a damsel in drag, Shakespeare must've rolled over in his (or Bacon's or Marlowe's) grave. (On the other hand, James Baldwin was probably laughing his buns off in *his* grave....)

I GUESS IT ALL WORKS ITSELF OUT IN THE END.

But What About the Men?

THEN, AS NOW, MEN WERE USELESS ORNAMENTS.

Until the end of the 18th century, the Tenor sang secondary roles and was lucky to get an aria to himself; the Bass was almost a non-entity.

The Italians (truly an understatement) eventually got over their hostility toward Tenors. They did such a good job of it that the Italian Stock Exchange now ranks Tenors between olive oil and cleavage as one of Italy's top three exports.

We're getting ahead of ourselves. (Behind ourselves too.)

Ferri

The first of the great Castrati was a dude named **Ferri** (1610-1680). He was born and trained in Italy but did most of his singing in Poland! (I don't make this stuff up, you know!) By the time he appeared in Italy to sing (1643), Ferri was so famous that the townspeople met him three miles outside the city and filled his carriage with flowers (a good thing).

> "What this noble singer expressed with his voice is beyond description. There was, to begin with, the purity of his voice and...the impact of the trills and the ease and grace with which he achieved every note. But beyond all that, after a very long, sustained and lovely passage beyond the lung capacity of any other singer, he would, without taking a breath, go into a very long and lovely trill and then into still another passage, more brilliant and beautiful than the first".
>
> **Bontempi**: *Istoria Musica*

The ARIA da CAPO

Opera's development was a collaboration between Composer and Singer—it was Ferri's spectacular singing that led to the **aria da capo**, one of the cornerstones on which Opera was built.

THE ARIA

ARIA DA CAPO:
An Aria in three parts; the second is in contrast to the first; and the third is a repetition of the first.
The popular song is a derivative of the *da capo* aria.

FARINELLI: Prozacking the King:

According to Opera legend, King Philip V of Spain was so bummed-out that he wouldn't wash, shave, dress, or act like a proper King. The Queen and her cabinet had tried all the traditional cures from leeches to Hail Marys, so the Queen, on a hunch, invited the famous castrato **Farinelli** (1705-1782) to sing a few tunes in "a room adjoining the King's apartment."

King Phil opened one eye during the first song, his other eye during the second song, and by the third song he was so moved by Farinelli's singing that he invited the famous gelding into his apartment and embraced him!

Farinelli did such a good job of Prozacking the king, that every day for 25 years he had to sing the royal bozo to sleep with the same four songs. In between gigs for the nervous king, Farinelli managed to start an Italian Opera company in Madrid.

After King Phil died (1762), Farinelli resumed his long delayed tour of Europe—but by then even he could see that the reign of the castrati was coming to an end.

THINGS WERE SO BAD THAT EVEN—GOD FORBID—WOMEN WERE BEGINNING TO APPEAR ONSTAGE.

As I sit here writing this book, a new movie, _Farinelli,_ is opening in New York. Farinelli's movie voice was created by mating a countertenor with a computer! The movie is part fact, all fiction, and pretty good except for the computer's singing.)

The First Women
& the Last Castrati

At first the Europeans were put off by the unnaturalness of women singing female roles but eventually they got used to it. (Two early sopranos, Bordoni and Cuzzoni, used to follow each other from city to city, sabotaging each other's performances!) By the time Velluti (one of the last great castrati) appeared in London in 1825, the British considered <u>him</u> rather freakish. It would take the Italians a few more years to get the message.

BUT WHEN THEY GOT IT, HONEY, THEY <u>REALLY</u> GOT IT!

Newton merely discovered the boring Law of Gravity; all Einstein did was come up with the squeaky little Law of Relativity; but it was the Italians—
I repeat: the Italians
—who invented the Tenor. The world had never heard anything like it.

We begin, naturally, by studying the Italian tenor, **B.C....**

B.C. = (Before Caruso)

Many B.C. singers made important contributions to the art, skill, and sport of singing Opera.

In the simplest terms, those contributions fell into two categories:

THOSE WHO CONTRIBUTED TO THE PURE SINGING OF OPERA;

AND THOSE WHO CONTRIBUTED TO THE ACTING.

The Un-Altered Tenors—Pure SINGERS

Spanish tenor **Manuel Garcia** (1775-1832) had a hell of a resume: He was one of the premier tenors of his time (Rossini and Donizetti wrote Operas for him); he fathered two prime time sopranos (Maria Malibran and Pauline Viardot-Garcia); he was one of the first people to "bring Opera to the natives" (he toured the U.S. in 1825); and he may have been the best singing teacher of all time (people still use the instruction manuals he wrote in the early 1800s—and his only competition for the #1 Voice Teacher of all time, Mathilde Marchesi, was one of his students).

Despite all that, Papa Garcia wasn't <u>famous</u> famous.

"A GUY SINGING A MALE ROLE...WHAT A FREAK."

TONITE

GARCIA

The reason: People had barely gotten used to the unnatural fact of women singing female roles—now, on top of that, they were expected to accept ungelded men in male roles! *Yick!*

68

RUBINI

Despite the fact that tenor **Giovanni Rubini** (1795-1854) was awkward, ugly, had an unmagnificent voice, and couldn't act, he was the first "normal" male singer to cop the kind of rock-star fame that the prima donnas and castrati enjoyed.

Rubini did have a couple things going for him: He was the first to use the fast **vibrato**. And most important of all, Rubini invented the **Italian sob**.

THINK ABOUT IT: NO SOB, NO CARUSO, NO GIGLI...NO OPERA?

Inventing the DRAMATIC Tenor

The tenor voice is considered the most unnatural—and the most thrilling—of all, so it's not surprising that tenors have generally been singers first and actors second (or not at all).

Adolphe Nourrit (1802-1839) was not your average tenor: He was an actor first, a singer second, and (if that isn't handicap enough) he was French. He was so good that the dozen-or-so Operas written expressly for him (by Rossini, Meyerbeer, Halevy, and Auber) literally *created* the repertoire for the dramatic tenor. Unfortunately, they also created the backdrop for his tragic end.

In 1837, the tenor Duprez made his debut at the French Opera (the place where Nourrit had reigned supreme for 12 years) in the role of Arnold in Rossini's <u>William Tell</u>—Nourrit's main role.

NOURRIT COULDN'T HANDLE IT. HE QUIT THE OPERA. TWO YEARS LATER, AT THE AGE OF 37, HE KILLED HIMSELF.

Gilbert-Louis Duprez (1806-1896) was the first to sing a high C "from the chest." (All the previous ones were "head tones.") How did it sound? An 1849 entry from tenor G. Roger's diary:

"Duprez, today, electrified us all.... How he hurled his guts into the audience's face! For those are no longer notes that one hears.... That's his own blood, his own life, that he is squandering to entice from the public those cries of 'Bravo!'"

Domenico Donzelli (1790-1873), Italy's first great dramatic tenor, was one of the first tomcats to sing high notes without using falsetto.

FALSETTO'S WHAT SMOKEY ROBINSON DOES.

Rossini hated the full-voiced high notes, but he was so impressed by Donzelli's singing that he wrote several Operas for the man.

Defining the BARITONE & BASS

Before **Antonio Tamburini** (1800-1876) and **Luigi Lablache** (1794-1858), men with deep voices not only "didn't get no respect," but they were lumped together into one indistinct category. Tamburini and Lablache defined the difference between a Baritone (Tamburini) and a Bass (Lablache). That opened the door for the "Verdi baritone"—the stud with high notes that rival the Tenor.

Inventing the DRAMATIC SOPRANO

Giuditta Pasta (1798-1865) was a dramatic soprano before there were any dramatic operas for her to sing. She was past her prime by the time Bellini and Donizetti wrote Operas intense enough to accomodate her acting. Critic Henry Pleasants compares "Pasta's imperfect and unruly voice" to Maria Callas.

  Maria Malibran (1808-1836), one of the first dramatic acting sopranos, toured the U.S. with her famous father Manuel Garcia in 1825. During that nine month tour, Malibran, age 17, sang virtually every day without holding back. The super-intense Malibran died at the age of 28. In the words of the British critic, Cholrley,

"She passed across the operatic stage like a comet."

Wilhemine Schroder-Devrient (1804-1860) pioneered the German (as opposed to the Italian) Dramatic Soprano. Schroder-Devrient was so intense she made the Italians seem Swedish. She would cry, scream, talk, rave, or do anything she pleased to turn up the dramatic heat. (Wagner said that seeing her in Beethoven's <u>Fidelio</u> made him decide to become a composer.) She may have been the most riveting actress ever to scream around an Opera stage—<u>and</u> one of the worst singers. When she tried her hand at Italian Opera, she was a graceless oaf. If you leave out the high notes and the fancy stuff like trills and cross-over dribbles, Italian bel canto Opera is so smooth that it sounds like it would sing itself.

Two Diametrically Opposed Approaches to the Art of Dramatic Singing

FAT CHANCE! NOT ONLY IS IT A BITCH TO SING, BUT THE PART THAT SOUNDS EASIEST (WHAT SINGERS CALL LEGATO— THE SEAMLESS CONNECT-ING OF NOTES) IS THE TOUGHEST.

The difference between Italian and German dramatic singing is more than a difference in language, it's a difference of style, attitude...I am tempted to say that it's the difference between a Kiss and a Punch in the Mouth, but that's going too far. (<u>Not</u> a lot too far; a <u>little</u> too far.)

German dramatic Opera is not so much *sung* as it is *declaimed.* ("Declaim" is a polite word for *shout* or *harangue.* To *harangue* [I had to look it up] is to make a "long, pompous speech characterized by strong feeling or vehement expression; a tirade. A *tirade* is a "long violent or blustering speech.")

Waaaay at the other end of the spectrum are the Italians, who (as one smartass put it) "want to sound beautiful even if the words are 'My mother is dying.'"

There is a universe between the German and Italian approaches to Opera. But it's an *interesting* universe, filled with passion and brilliance and beauty on both sides.

Inventing the MEZZO

Pauline Viardot-Garcia (1821-1910), Garcia's "other" daughter, set the standard for the modern Mezzo Soprano through her work with the French composer Meyerbeer. Viardot was both a great actress and a bravura singer. If there was any complaint about her, it was that she overdid the fioritura.

Fioritura = a singer's embellishment of the written aria, often improvised, and considered part of every good singer's arsenal until composers began complaining—then insisting—that singers sing the aria <u>as written</u>, *period!* *(NOTE: Later, when singers like Joan Sutherland, Beverly Sills, and Marilyn Horne talk about returning to the art of "Embellishment," this is it!)*

The NIGHTINGALES

German coloratura soprano **Henriette Sontag** (1806-1854) made her Opera debut at age 15. Her voice was clear, bright, high, and small. Sontag was one of the few singers who could challenge the Italians in their own roles—which in those days meant mostly Rossini. "My God," Malibran said when she first heard Sontag, "why does she sing so beautifully?"

Jenny Lind (1820-1887), the "Swedish Nightingale," was a bitch who acted like a saint. Despite the fact that she never sang in either Italy or France — "for *moral reasons"!*—she may have been the most popular coloratura soprano of her time. And if that isn't weird enough, she toured America with P.T. Barnum. (Yes, <u>that</u> P.T. Barnum). She had a beautiful, girlish voice, great high notes, amazing breath control and a Little-Bo-Peep act that couldn't quite hide the sanctimonious bigot she really was.

A mere Diva would be a relief after that little witch.

DIVA? Did somebody say

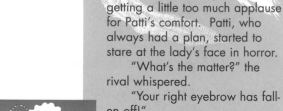

...the lord removed the Tenor's rib, turned it into a Diva, and sayeth unto them, "Go forth, be bitchy and multiply."

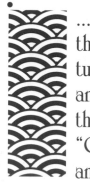

Adelina Patti (1843-1919) was a pretty great singer and a very great Diva. In Patti's day, Divas wore fake hair, fake boobs, fake smiles, and, of course, false eyebrows...

Patti was a singer, *period*. She couldn't act her way out of a paper bag (whatever that means). As far as she was concerned, acting was the last refuge for second-rate singers. And if you weren't sure if she was a first-rate singer, just ask her!

One time, a rival soprano was getting a little too much applause for Patti's comfort. Patti, who always had a plan, started to stare at the lady's face in horror.

"What's the matter?" the rival whispered.

"Your right eyebrow has fallen off!"

The embarrassed rival turned her back to the public and removed her left eyebrow. Unfortunately, there had been nothing wrong with the right one—and the lady played the rest of the act with one of her eyebrows missing.

Opera fanatics love to tell about the time the suits from Gramophone finally persuaded Patti, age 61, to make a recording. Playing her records back to her was risky—whatever age she claimed that *she* was, her <u>voice</u> was 61 years old. When her records were released, many of her fans were disappointed. Not Patti. When she finally heard her own voice, she was overcome with emotion. Blowing kisses into the playback horn, she cried,

"WHAT A VOICE! WHAT AN ARTIST! NOW I UNDERSTAND EVERYTHING!"

The Queen of DIVA

Dame Nellie Melba (1861-1931), never the shy type, called herself the Queen of Song. The Australian soprano was witty, bitchy, and power hungry (those were her *good* qualities).

But she could sing. Mary Garden, a rival soprano who had every reason to hate her, said of Melba's high C in a performance of <u>La Boheme</u>, that "it came over like a star...and went out into the infinite...My God, how beautiful it was!"

There's a famous story involving Melba, tenor Jean de Reszke, and . . . I'll let Melba tell it:

I shall never forget an evening when I was singing with Jean de Reszke [Chicago,1896] in *Romeo and Juliet*..and before I knew what had happened I saw clambering up over the footlights a man with staring eyes and the face of a lunatic, coming towards me.

It *was* a lunatic, a man who had in some way or other escaped from his asylum and had obtained entry to the house. For a moment everybody was paralysed. And then Jean came to the rescue. He ran forward, drawing his stage sword from its sheath and waving it fiercely in the man's face. The man looked as though he might give fight—and if he had done so I don't know what would have happened, for he was a powerful fellow and a theatrical sword is not a very good weapon against the strength of a maniac.

DAME NELLIE MELBA: *MELODIES AND MEMORIES*, 1925

Jean de Reszke (1850-1925) was not only a brave guy, he was also one of the greatest Italian tenors of all time—despite the fact that he was Polish and specialized in French Opera!

He also became one of the great *German* tenors when he did the unthinkable and became a Wagnerian *heldentenor* late in his career. DeReszke was a hard act to follow.

That's where the little fat guy from Naples comes in...

Caruso, when he was an unknown tenor, auditioned for Puccini by singing "Che gelida manina," from La Boheme.
Puccini said,
"Who sent you—God?"

Scene 13:

Mr. Caruso

Why, you may reasonably wonder, should Opera singers be divided into BEFORE & AFTER CARUSO— with Uncle Enrico in the middle like the Mason-Dixon Line?

Caruso may have been the greatest Opera singer of all time (or the greatest tenor) (or the greatest Italian tenor). You can argue about that till your fake eyebrows fall off; it's a matter of taste that even you will change your mind about several times.

That is NOT the reason Mr. Caruso is the dividing line.

These are the reasons:
1. He changed the art of Opera singing.
2. He changed the art of being an Opera singer.
3. But above all, because from Caruso onward, you can hear the singers we're talking about.

(We're not talking about anything mystical here, dude—they were recorded!) One thing you have to love about Caruso was that he broke so many of the stereotypes.

Breaking the Sterotypes

Take, for example, the jive about Opera being a rich dude's sport...

Enrico Caruso (1873-1921), arguably the greatest Opera singer of all time, was a little fat guy from the slums of Naples. He was the 18th of 21 children, only three of whom lived beyond infancy. As a boy, he worked in a machine shop to help his family survive; evenings, he sang on streetcorners to earn money for singing lessons.

Caruso made his debut in Naples in 1894 in an Opera that not only flopped—the damn thing *disappeared!* He was 21. Two years later, he materialized at Puccini's crib. Two years after that, he created the role of Loris in **Giordano**'s Opera **Fedora**. Two years after that, he made his debut at LaScala, the Opera house in Milan where they make you "keep singing it until you get it right." (He got it right the first time.)

HIS MASTER'S VOICE

In 1902, one of the pointmen from Gramophone heard Caruso wailin' up a storm at LaScala and was so astounded that he offered the Tenor $500 to record ten arias. The head office wired back, FEE EXORBITANT FORBID YOU TO RECORD. The guy ignored his bosses, and the records made a fortune—that, my babies, is how supernatural the chubby brother's voice was! That big, lush, perfectly focused, voice of his was damn near the only voice in town that could move the Flintstone technology of the old Gramophone and Victrola recording machines. Other beautiful voices came out squeaky or muffled; Caruso's voice sounded like God was singing in your living room!

Caruso's recordings are **not** considered "collectors' items" in any serious sense simply because he sold zillions of them! Caruso was a *pop* recording artist—Elvis the Pelvis Caruso!

77

The Down-to-Earth DIVO

In 1903, at age 30, Caruso made his American debut at the Met(ropolitan Opera House) in New York. Americans loved him. Not only was there that Voice, but he fit in perfectly with America's notions (or fantasies?) of democractic equality. The Greatest Singer in the World—and he's a Nice Guy! Talk about breaking stereotypes. Nice, likeable, warm, generous (to a fault)— even approachable. He was the perfect American success story. So what if he was Italian? Everybody in America is something!

Yes, but...How Did He Change the Art of SINGING Opera?

Caruso was to singing what Verdi was to composing: He made singing more direct, simpler, less fancy, more blatantly emotional. He premiered many of the most famous tenor roles in Operas by Puccini, Giordano, and Cilea and his performances in verismo Operas (e.g., Pagliacci) are still the standards by which tenors are judged. According to some smart cookies, what made Caruso's voice so unique (and gave it that magnificent organ-like resonance) was that his "chest voice" was as beautiful as his "head voice." (Pop music equivalents: "falsetto" = Smokey Robinson; "head voice" = Tony Williams of The Platters; "chest voice" = late R&:B great, Jackie Wilson.) The Caruso sob is also definitive.

YOU CAN KNOCK OFF THE SOBBING ACT ERNIE...I'M NOT LETTING YOU STAY THE NIGHT...

On the OTHER Hand

Stephen Zucker (of <u>Opera Fanatic</u> magazine and radio show) strongly implies that Caruso, in many ways, had a negative impact on the Art of Singing Opera. According to Zucker (and the man is a veritable asylum of knowledge), Caruso was the first to sing without "dynamic modulation" (mixing loud and soft singing). Caruso was the first to sing almost exclusively *forte* (loud).

My best guess is that Zucker finds Caruso's singing pretty damned beautiful, but he laments the fact that a century's-worth of tenors have followed him like sheep.

(I CAN GET NEXT TO THAT.)

Music to DIE For

Caruso stayed at the Met for 18 years, where he sang over 600 performances in 40 different roles. So everyone was surprised to see him in trouble in a performance of L'Elisir d'Amore at the Brooklyn Academy of Music on December 11, 1920. Caruso was spitting blood with every phrase, but he kept singing. His doctor hysterically waved at him to stop, but he kept singing. Finally, the General Manager of the Met was called in to stop the performance. Everybody in the audience knew that they'd witnessed an extraordinary act. But what did it mean? One of the most gifted men the world has ever known was risking his gift, his Voice—maybe even his life—to sing an Opera.

Can the music be that important?

Two days after his Brooklyn performance, Caruso sang in La Forza del Destino. He sounded as good as ever; he tried to put the pain out of his mind. He sang La Juive on Christmas Eve, but he couldn't hide the pain on his face. The next day, during a Christmas party, the pain attacked again. It was diagnosed as pleurisy.

He had an operation. He lost weight, He died.

Can the music be that important?

Is there something going on here that we don't understand?

Yes. We'll get to it.

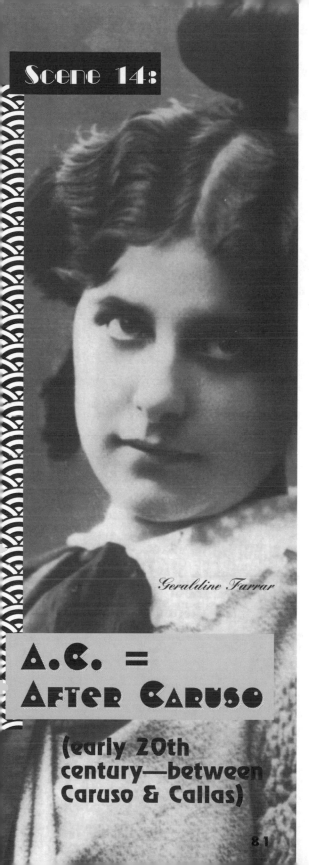

Scene 14:

Geraldine Farrar

A.C. = After Caruso

(early 20th century—between Caruso & Callas)

"Sex is repressed Opera."
Sigmund Floyd

There were so many fine singers at the turn of the century that the period between 1890 and 1920 is called the "Golden Age" of singing.

American superstar soprano **Geraldine Farrar** (1882-1967) was pretty, she was often paired with Caruso, and she was a better singer than she's usually given credit for. (Her recording of "Vissi d'arte" from Puccini's <u>Tosca</u> has a rhythmic drive that nobody else managed.)

Mary Garden (1874-1967) was born in Scotland, raised in Chicago, and specialized in French Opera.

Titta Ruffo (1877-1953) was the Baritone Caruso. They didn't exactly avoid each other, but it was no accident that Ruffo made his American career in Chicago and they recorded together only once—the duet from Verdi's <u>Otello</u>. Caruso's voice, always magnificent, became darker and more baritonal as he aged; By the time he sang that duet with Ruffo, you could barely tell them apart.

The great Irish tenor **John McCormack** (1884-1943) was as unlike Caruso as a tenor could be—McCormack's voice was high and thin and very Irish—but he and Caruso dug each other so much that each called the other "the world's greatest tenor."

Amelita Galli-Curci (1882-1963) was a tiny, hummingbird-voiced coloratura who could sing circles around the Big Mamas. (There is a bizarre recording alternating Galli-Curci's little flute-like singing voice with her 75-year-old croaky speaking voice.)

Speaking of big mamas, **Ernestine Schumann-Heink** (1861-1936), was an extremely big mama, a contralto who was born in Czechoslovakia, studied music in Germany, and became a proud American citizen. Ms. Schumann-Heink was a life-loving, earth-mother roughly the size of footballer William "The Refrigerator" Perry. About the only thing that'd tick her off is if you implied that she hadn't lost her German accent. (She made a beautiful recording of "Danny Boink.") One day the lovable linebacker boogied into an American drugstore for a few staples.

"I'd like some powder please," says she.
"Mennen's?" asks the clerk.
"No. Vimmen's."
"And would you like it scented?"
"No, I'll take it vit me."

Always be Sincere...

The Italian tenor **Benjamino Gigli** (1890-1957) is generally considered Caruso's successor, although he was much different in voice and personality. Caruso's voice was always "studly," whereas Gigli's voice was not only smaller, but a little sissified. Caruso, even though his sobs were sometimes over the edge, had what contemporary tenor Francisco Araiza calls "a tear in the voice," whereas Gigli is clearly an impostor. Gigli is famous for many things—for having one of the most beautiful natural voices, for "covering" the voice (using the sound "aw" instead of "ah"), but what Gigli is most famous for in <u>my</u> heart is his Magnificent Phoniness. Gigli was so moved by his own singing that he would stand on stage, clutching his heart, sobbing for several minutes after he had finished his aria.

> **A**lways be sincere, even if you don't mean it.
> —Harry S. Truman

It's NATURAL

Giovanni Martinelli (1885-1969) is usually considered next in the line of great Italian tenors. Opera lore has it that he was scheduled to replace an ailing Gigli halfway through the Opera <u>Andrea Chenier.</u> Gigli, who was in resplendent voice despite his illness, sang Chenier's *"Improviso"* aria. Martinelli said, "You expect me to go out there and sing after *that!* "

...a very young performer, unexperienced in the perils of the profession...made an appearance in company with the great Giovanni Martinelli. Both flattered and awed by the veteran's concern for her well-being during an embrace, she discovered—to her maidenly surprise—that she was encountering a rigid male organ poking her in the groin. As she instinctively recoiled, he squeezed her hand in a gesture of reassurance, and said, "Pardona, signorina. E'naturale!" ("No need to get all bent out of shape, lady. It's natural!")
IRVING KOLODIN: *THE OPERA OMNIBUS*

To Vibrate or NOT to...

Aureliano Pertile (1885-1952) was a star at LaScala and Toscanini's favorite Tenor, but he never caught on in America or England because of his fast vibrato (the British called it "bleating").

Tenor **Giacomo Lauri-Volpi** (1892-1979) also had the characteristic Italian vibrato, but he sang at New York's Metropolitan Opera for over ten years (from 1923 to 1934).

Tito Schipa (1890-1965) was a fine light-voiced tenor, despite the fact that he didn't have a great voice or great high notes. All the poor guy had were brains and elegance.

BEAUTY and the BASS

Spanish mezzo **Conchita Supervia** (1895-1936) was the last of the great vibratos. Her career was not hurt by the facts that she had a beautiful face, a great body, sang her first *Carmen* at age 15, and sang the hell out of Rossini.

Maria Jeritza (1887-1982), star of the Vienna Opera, didn't have a thing going for her except a gorgeous voice, great acting ability, and a body that looks fat in pictures but apparently had Puccini sniffing around her like an old hound dog.

Ezio Pinza (1892-1957), one of the great Italian basses from the 1920s to the 1940s, couldn't read music, loved the ladies, and had one of the most magnificent voices ever.

Feodor Chaliapin (1873-1938), the first *Russian* "basso profundo" to become internationally famous, single-handedly made <u>Boris Godunov</u> part of the standard repetory of Opera houses all over the world. He was a great singer and an even better actor.

Claudia Muzio (1889-1936) was a passionate singing actress, one of the first "modern" verismo singers. She had a beautiful, smoky voice, a strong personality, and brains.

WAGNERIAN HeldenHonkies

Lotte Lehmann (1888-1976) was one of the great German sopranos of the first half of the century. She originated many of Richard Strauss' soprano roles and she sang with tenderness even when impersonating one of Wagner's helmeted Heldenmamas.

> **Frida Leider** (1888-1975), another glorious Wagnerian soprano, had a bright, beautiful, youthful sounding voice compared to most Wagnerian sopranos. She sang the Fat-Lady roles with a voice as clear as a...clear as a...clear as a...

Friedrich Schorr (1888-1953) was one of the greatest Wagnerian bass-baritones of all time. His huge, vibrant voice glowered over Wagner's zillion-piece-orchestra like rolling thunder.

Many Jews despise Wagner, a big mouth, unrepentant antiSemite.

Although he didn't exactly advertise it, Friedrich Schorr was Jewish. Maybe he felt that his presence was the best revenge: Schorr's signature role was Wotan, King of the Gods.

Kirsten Flagstad (1895-1962) was nobody's favorite singer until, <u>at age 39</u>, she tackled Opera's toughest female role: the mighty Brunnhilde. She became <u>the</u> Wagnerian soprano of the 1930s-40s. Flagstad's performances with Melchoir saved the Metropolitan Opera from collapse during the Great Depression of the 1930s.

Speaking of Mr. Melchoir...

If a singer's irreplaceability is the ultimate standard of greatness, then Danish Tenor **Lauritz Melchoir** (1890-1973) is the greatest singer of all time. Melchoir sang all of Wagner's most brutal Heldentenor roles, and in the process, showed us what beautiful music they were. He was also the top partner for all three of the Wagnerian

super-ladies listed above (and others). Since Melchoir's retirement, nobody—and I mean <u>nobody</u>—has stepped in to fill the "helden-gap" he left.

(Siegfried, where are you?)

Austrian tenor **Richard Tauber** (1891-1948) started out in Opera but made his greatest impact in Operetta. He had a unique voice that he used with outrageous flair...and he wore a monacle!

Rosa Ponselle (1897-1981 was born in Connecticut and discovered by Caruso. She became one of the great Verdi sopranos and set the standard for the role of Norma...until Callas came along.

Marian Anderson (1903) was born in Philadelphia, where her father sold coal and her mother worked as a maid. In 1929, she went to Europe on a scholarship and met the impresario Sol Hurok, who signed her for a concert in Salzburg (Aug., 1935). Just before she was ready to go on, she was told that Toscanini, the Pope of conductors, might attend. She panicked. After the concert, Toscanini came backstage to talk to her but she was so nervous she didn't hear a word he said. After Toscanini left, others in the room told Anderson what he'd said: "Yours is a voice one hears once in a hundred years."

It would be another 20 years before she would make her debut at the Metropolitan Opera. During that time, a lot would happen, including World War II and Maria Callas.

WOULD YOU CARE FOR SOME GROUND PEPPER WITH YOUR WORDS?

P.C.= Post Callas

—mid-to-late 20th century—

Maria Callas (1923-1977) was born in Brooklyn to Greek parents. Shortly before World War II, her mother took her to live in Greece, where Maria studied voice with an unspectacular teacher and made an unremarkable debut in 1938.

Then something happened. It's as if, one night in her sleep she was visited by Rossini, Bellini, Verdi, Wagner, Puccini and a couple dozen of the world's greatest prehistoric singers...and...they put a computer chip into her head? Or something? I know the Rules; I know things like that can't happen. But it's *as if* they happened!

Suddenly, in 1947, this unremarkable girl makes a strong debut in Verona. In 1949, this ordinary girl sings Brunnhilde (in <u>Die Walkure</u>) and Elvira (in <u>I Puritani</u>)— back to back!

(Is the girl retarded? Doesn't she know that's impossible?)

Where had she learned it? Her vocal quality—not only the natural sound, but the way in which she used it—was so unusual that she practically had to barge into opera.

"That woman [Maria Callas] will never sing at La-Scala," Antonio Ghiringhelli told Gian Carlo Menotti.

"Never! Never!"

ETHAN MORDDEN:
OPERA ANECDOTES

Even more astonishing, this Greek girl from Brooklyn is telling the baddest conductors in Italy how Rossini should be sung! And Bellini, Donizetti, Verdi—you name it. The woman is clearly nuts. She acts like she just got back from the 18th century!

In 1951, Callas sang <u>Norma</u> at LaScala. She was so good it was scary. But she was still nuts! In Brazil, she found her name removed from posters advertising her upcoming <u>Tosca</u>, so she beat the hell out of the Opera House's impresario! In those days, Callas weighed over 200 lbs, so she carried a serious wallop.

Madame Butterball

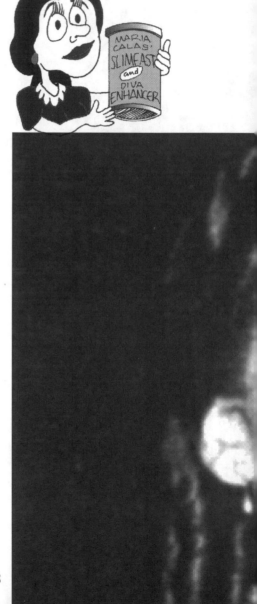

It was around that time that conductor Tulio Serafin told Callas that her large body was retarding her career. Maria protested that she wasn't that big. The great baritone Tito Gobbi tactlessly pointed out a nearby scale. Callas weighed herself, took off her coat, weighed herself again, then stormed away.

What Gobbi saw a year later, he couldn't believe: She had lost over 100 lbs. and she was beautiful, but those things one accepts. What shocked Gobbi was that this new Callas was not the old one transformed; she was, or seemed to be, an entirely new person. Everything that was <u>not</u> the diva had been burned away.

The Great Ugly Voice

Callas' voice was so odd it's a wonder she ever got past the lobby of a big time Opera house. But it was unmistakeable. Conductor Carlo Maria Guilini called her "the Great Ugly Voice." She considered it a compliment; he meant it as one.

Between 1950 and the early 1960s, Callas revived a couple dozen dead Operas, revived—and redeemed—the entire genre of Bel Canto Operas, changed the performing of <u>all</u> Opera, and raised the sights of every Opera singer who followed her. All that in a career whose prime lasted barely ten years. After the early 1960s, the wobble became wobblier and the high notes screechier.

Of course, along the way, she also dissed soprano Renata Tebaldi, pissed off the President of Italy (she walked out after Act One of <u>Norma</u> when he was in the audience), cancelled performances, and feuded with anyone dumb enough to get in her way.

Then one day the greatest, baddest Opera singer since Caruso met the rich butterfly collector, Aristotle Onassis. He pinned her, told her to give up Opera. She did. He married Jackie Kennedy in 1968. (If only she hadn't given up Opera, we could have hated Onassis with a nice clear conscience; but she did, so we can't.) Officially, Callas didn't die until 1977.

Author's Note: After I wrote that last line, I found myself looking up Billie Holiday's birth-&-death years, half expecting them to be the same as Callas'. (They aren't.) I cannot understand one without the other.

When Callas sang, she put everything on the line.
Did we expect her to love any other way?

The La Scala Gang

The recordings from LaScala during the Callas years set the standard for other Opera houses. La Scala had great conductors like Giulini and Serafin, big time movie directors like Visconti and Zeffirelli, and enough fine singers to fill three Opera houses. Two of the greatest La Scala singers were Gobbi and di Stefano.

Baritone Tito Gobbi (1915-1984) made his debut in 1937, but his career didn't really fly until after the war (WWII). By the 1950s, he was in demand all over the world. He sang and acted with equal suavity; he could be funny (Figaro in <u>The Barber of Seville</u>), brutal (Scarpia in <u>Tosca</u>), or tender (Rodrigo in <u>Don Carlos</u>). He sang with Callas in many of her best roles—especially <u>Tosca</u>.

The Italian Tenor Giuseppe di Stefano (b.1921) was Callas' most constant partner. He started out as a popular crooner before he committed his smooth tonsils to Opera. He made his debut in Italy in 1946, and at the Met in 1948. It would be wrong to treat di Stephano as merely Callas' partner; he was a fine singer in his own right. Supertenor Jussi Bjoerling once said, "Di Stefano could be the best of all of us if he put his mind to it."

Jussi Bjoerling (1911-1960) started singing professionally with his father and brothers at the age of six. He made his Operatic debut in Stockholm in 1930. Caruso's widow said that Bjoerling's was the only voice she'd ever heard that reminded her of Caruso.

That made a lot of people nervous:

...in 1931...the great Feodor Chaliapin appeared [in Stockholm, Sweden] as a guest artist singing Mephistopheles [in Gounod's Faust]. The tenor on this occasion was the legendary Jussi Bjoerling, then at the beginning of his career; throughout the performance, Chaliapin noticed that the young tenor had a splendid voice and might provide too much competition for him in this crucial final scene. When the time came for them all to belt it out, Chaliapin simply removed his competition by swirling his cape around the young tenor and covering him from the sight (and sound) of the audience!

STEPHEN M. STROFF: OPERA—AN INFORMAL GUIDE

Early in 1960, Bjoerling had a heart attack at Covent Garden just before the curtain of La Boheme. Bjoerling, reputed to be a man of immense physical strength, insisted on singing because the Queen of England was in the audience. He died a few months later. It was the year that Leontyne Price made her Met debut.

Five years earlier, in 1955—twenty years after Toscanini had raved about her—Met Opera General Manager Rudolph Bing defied the Met's whitebread Board of Directors and invited **Marian Anderson** to sing at the Met. She was still a fine singer, but she was well past her prime, so Opera lovers never did get to hear the *real* Marian Anderson.

AND THEY'RE _STILL_ TRYING TO FIGURE OUT WHICH RUDOLPH BING IS THE REAL RUDOLPH BING.

Rudolph the Blue Nosed impresario

The Rudolph Bing that Callas fans still despise did the unforgivable: During Callas' prime (the 50s and early 60s), she sang at La Scala, Covent Garden, the Paris Opera, the Lyric Opera of Chicago...she sang damn near everywhere in the world except the Met. Actually, she sang at the Met *twice* during her prime. She was scheduled to sing more performances, but Bing fired her because there was "no room at the Met for a Prima Donna." Opera lovers saw through Bing's doubletalk: What he really meant was that there was room at the Met for *only* one Prima Donna— Rudolph Bing. Bing the Bitchy was famous for his wisecracks: Someone remarked,

"[CONDUCTOR] GEORGE SZELL IS HIS OWN WORST ENEMY."

"NOT WHILE I'M ALIVE,"

Bing replied.

As long as we're doing bitchy remarks: After hearing Tebaldi, Callas said, "What a lovely voice! But who the hell cares?" However...

You don't take the trouble to dump on someone who isn't a threat. **Renata Tebaldi** (b.1922) grabbed some serious international fame when Toscanini chose her for the reopening of La Scala in 1946. By 1955, she had sung in all the major Opera houses. Tebaldi was a tame actress with a big luscious voice. Opera lovers are like sports fans: If you love Jordan, you feel obliged to hate Barkley, and vice versa. Tebaldi fans and Callas fans were like rival New York gangs, complete with occasional fistfights.

Franco Corelli (b.1923), who sang with both Callas and Tebaldi, didn't have much formal voice training but he had a big, ringing tenor voice with great high notes. Unfortunately, Corelli lived in such mortal terror of his own high notes that his anxiety over performing shortened his career. They called him "Golden calves"...

The "mature" American tenor Richard Tucker tried to ignore the Opera house flunkies fawning over the studly new tenor, Franco Corelli. Sensing Tucker's discomfort, the disgustingly handsome, magnificent voiced Corelli, told Tucker that he admired the old dude's version of an aria from Puccini's <u>Tosca</u>. Corelli asked Tucker's advice on singing the piece.

Tucker, whose toupee looked like a pancake that had been dropped on his head, said, "To sing it right, Franco, you have to be Jewish."

Richard Tucker (1913-1975) was many people's second or third-favorite tenor. He sang at the Met for 30 years and never gave anything less than an all-out performance.

Which brings us to **Mario** "Iron Lungs" **DelMonaco** (1915-1982). Del Monaco was <u>the</u> great Italian Dramatic Tenor of the 40s and 50s —if not, of all modern time. His specialty was the title role in Verdi's <u>Otello</u>. He had a fierce and beautiful voice, was almost as good-looking as Corelli, skipped sex before performances like a prizefighter, and sometimes got so carried away that he shouted his lines instead of singing them!

They say that Swedish soprano **Birgit Nilsson** (b.1918) didn't drown out Franco Corelli when they sang <u>Turandot</u> together because she liked him. Corelli had a huge voice, so that would seem ridiculous unless you heard Nilsson sing. She was, without doubt, <u>the</u> Wagnerian soprano of the 50s, 60s, and part of the 70s.

HER HUGE RINGING VOICE ROSE ABOVE EVEN THE LARGEST ORCHESTRAS.

German Soprano Elisabeth Schwarzkopf (b.1915) made her debut in Berlin in 1938. She specialized in Mozart and Richard Strauss. Her interpretation of the Marshallin in Strauss' <u>Der Rosenkavalier</u> is still considered definitive.

Leontyne Price (b.1927) was such a magnificent singer that it is hard to imagine her *not* being an enormous success, but racism does have a way of making people deaf, dumb, blind, and stupid—so we thank Marian Anderson for making Leontyne Price possible. Ms. Price was the first African American Opera singer to make an international reputation. She was born in Mississippi, studied at New York's Julliard, and became the top Verdi soprano of the 60s, 70s, and part of the 80s.

Australian soprano **Joan Sutherland** (b.1926) had a voice as big as a Wagnerian soprano and as flexible as a coloratura. She and her husband, conductor Richard Bonynge took the Bel Canto revival in a "Rossinian" direction. Rossini believed that singers and conductors should <u>not</u> treat the composer's <u>written</u> score like the Bible, but that each singer should modifiy the music to suit her own voice and temperament. Sutherland and Bonynge started the movement in the 60s. Others, like Beverly Sills and Marilyn Horne, took up the cause.

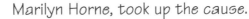

Richard Bonynge, Sutherland's husband and voice coach, "tricked" her into developing her spectacular high notes by telling her she was singing a B-flat when in fact, she was singing a C, D, and on up into the stratosphere.

Where Sutherland was an atypical *big voiced* coloratura, **Beverly Sills** (b.1929) was the traditional *small voiced* type. She was a smart singer but by the time she hit major fame, her voice had lost a bit of its bloom. After she quit singing, Sills, the good natured, hearty-laughing lady next door, became the head of the New York City Opera,

AND ONE OF OPERA'S BEST AMBASSADORS.

If Opera singers had a shootout at the OK Corral to see who could sing higher and lower and faster and slower than anyone else, I'd put my money on **Marilyn Horne** (b.1929). She may be the greatest razzle dazzle coloratura mezzo soprano ever recorded! And she's been singing since the 1950s, when her voice was "loaned" to Dorothy Dandridge in the movie, <u>Carmen Jones</u>.

Jessye Norman's (b.1945) strengths are so obvious that you wonder why the Met didn't hire her until 1983, when <u>she was 38 years old</u>! In her debut season at the Met, she sang the parts of both Cassandra and Dido in <u>Les Troyens</u>, and in the process she made *me* like that bum Berlioz. I have a theory: No matter how much weight Jessye Norman gains/loses, her face stays exactly the same; my theory is that she's a skinny lady hiding behind a cardboard cutout of a great big woman.

Three Tenors

For all I know, you live on Mars and you've never heard of "Air" Pavarotti and Kareem Abdul Domingo, two of the greatest players the world has ever known...let alone Clyde the Glide Carreras.

Tenor **Placido Domingo** (b.1941) was born in Spain, trained in Mexico, and sings everything. I mean _everything_! Verdi, Wagner, Offenbach, Mozart, Berlioz—the list is endless. He's one of the smartest singers in the world—and one of the few Opera singers who've actually improved with age. In the 80s, he began conducting—he's good at that too. (Maybe we could talk him into running for President!) He even, God forbid, seems sane!

DID HE REALLY SING WITH JOHN DENVER, OR WAS THAT ONE OF MY BAD DREAMS?

In 1963, **Luciano Pavarotti** (b.1935) was called in as a last minute substitute for Giuseppe di Stefano in a Covent Garden (London) production of La Boheme. The next day's London Times read, "Discovery of great new Italian tenor." In 1965, he was invited to tour with Joan Sutherland. In 1967, he sang the Verdi Requiem with Leontyne Price, at La Scala, conducted by Herbert von Karajan. His first debut at the Met (in 1968) was a disaster—he had the Hong Kong flu. He returned to the Met In 1972, singing Donizetti's Daughter of the Regiment, which included an impossible aria with nine high Cs. It put him on the cover of Time magazine...and the rest is history.

TIME

Spanish Tenor **Jose Carreras** (b.1946) had a beautiful voice and looked like a movie star, so no one was surprised when he began to get "famouser and famouser." Then, in 1985, he was stricken with leukemia. After months of treatment, including a bone marrow transplant, he recovered. With incredible patience and perseverance, Carreras worked his way back to singing. The voice, after he recovered, was not the same—

it wobbled like a wagon on a cobblestone street—but you had to respect the man and the guts it took.

In the spring of 1990, Carreras had the idea of organizing a concert to celebrate the end of the Italia '90 World Cup. He knew that his buddies Pavarotti and Domingo were great football fans (what Americans call "soccer"), so he invited them to join him. On July 7, 1990, The Three Tenors sang at the Baths of Caracalla in Rome. Their concert was televised all over the world, it has become the best selling Opera video ever, and it's already spawned a sequel—"Son of Three Tenors"...

OR SOMETHING LIKE THAT.

The time for talk has
ended , Grasshopper.
It'za time to listen.

ACT THREE:

LISTENING TO Opera

pie - tà,

re è un cer

è un cer

re è un ce

Scene 16:

LISTENING TO OPERA:

the way it's REALLY Done

The usual bookish advice on listening to Opera is about as realistic as a Rambo movie. I know dozens of people who, like me, have become "converts" to Opera. We all began listening to Opera in the same way. It's easy, it's fun, and it's <u>natural</u>.

RULE #1: IGNORE THE CONVENTIONAL ADVICE ON LISTENING TO OPERA.

The conventional advice is:

 Listen to the entire Opera once or twice

 Read the entire Libretto (as you listen to the Opera)

 Go to the entire Opera house

Most people didn't do that much homework in school, so they certainly aren't going to do it now. That may eventually browbeat you into "appreciating" Opera, but it kills any possibility of loving it! Opera is a madman's (or madwoman's) art.

IF YOU APPROACH IT WITH SANITY, YOU MISS THE WHOLE POINT OF IT!

If we resist our passions, it is more due to their weakness than to our strength.

..LA ROCHEFOUCAULD

An intense feeling carries with it its own universe.

..ALBERT CAMUS

OR, TO PUT THAT ANOTHER WAY:

"Too much of a good thing can be wonderful."

..MAE WEST

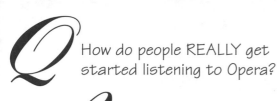

Q How do people REALLY get started listening to Opera?

A It's the same way you get started listening to "normal" music when you don't have anybody standing over you with a stick:

You listen to S<small>INGERS</small>—not Composers—and you judge the singers the same way you judge singers in regular music: from your soul, your senses, your <u>taste</u>.

YOUR TASTE, NOT SOME CRITIC'S.

You listen to <u>Songs</u>—or A<small>RIAS</small>—not entire Operas. It may be months—or years!—before you listen to an entire Opera. You do it when it seems natural—when you <u>feel</u> like doing it—not when someone says you <u>should</u> do it. Opera is music, not medicine.

You listen primarily to singers' Opera—I<small>TALIAN</small> Opera—not German (I hear the Music Police banging down my door!)—

then

...compare, compare, compare...

LEST THE CRITICAL TYPES GET THEIR NOSES OUT OF JOINT OVER MY HERESY, I'LL DEAL WITH NO. 3 FIRST.

Listen to *Italian* Opera Not German

On the surface, the quote below merely records the first appearance in English of the Italian term "Bel canto"...

"The Oxford English Dictionary gives the date of its first appearance in English as 1908....citing an article in the New York Daily Chronicle about the <u>complaints of music critics</u> that '<u>audiences do not want Wagner</u>' and that '<u>the public flocks to the Italian bel canto.</u>'"

Henry Pleasants—
The Great Singers

MY EMPHASIS.

SLAM!

Just beneath the surface, three points are made:

AUDIENCES DON'T WANT WAGNER, THEY DO WANT ITALIAN BEL CANTO—

AND THOSE TWO FACTS IRRITATE THE HELL OUT OF MUSIC CRITICS.

Therefore, RULE #2 is...

Ignore the CRITICS

A critic is a guy who makes a living looking down on things. Some generous people do it for free. Their entire personality consists of looking down their noses at everything!

> **I CRITICIZE, THEREFORE I AM!**

They play it safe.

I am the opposite...

"I'm a true adorer of life,
and if I can't reach as high as
the face of it,
I plant my kiss somewhere
further down."
SAUL BELLOW: HENDERSON THE RAIN KING

Cheap thrills, expensive thrills—I'll take them all. (Man cannot live on negative energy alone, Grasshopper.) Critics can bitch all they like, but that won't change the fact that virtually every new listener to Opera, listens primarily to the <u>singing</u>. And anyone who listens to Opera for the singing, listens to Italian Opera.

It really is (almost) that simple.

(Sorry—this is real life: everything has an almost in it!)

Of course there are German, French, (et cetera) singers and Operas that should be included in any survey of Opera, but if you want a rule for beginning listeners that holds true 90% of the time, it's simple: Pay attention to what the critics say— and do the opposite! When it comes to Opera, it's as if the critics have decided that Ecstasy is a danger that must be stamped out at any cost.

There's a story they tell about Verdi...

A Great Critic visited Verdi as he was putting the finishing touches on Il Trovatore.

"What do you think of this?" Verdi asked him, playing the Anvil Chorous.

"Trash," announced the Great Critic, for he loved only the finest things.

"Now try this," said Verdi, offering the Miserere.

"What rubbish!" the Great Critic observed, for his nuanced sensibility could accept only the most profound art.

"One last test," said Verdi. He presented the tenor's aria, "Di quella pira."

"It's beastly," said the Critic, for anything less than nobility made him shudder.

Verdi rose from the piano and embraced the Great Critic in momentous joy.

"What is the meaning of this?" asked the Great Critic.

"My dear friend," Verdi told him, "I have been writing a popular opera—an opera for the public, not for the purists and classicists and solemn judges, like you. If you liked this music, no one else would. But your distaste assures me of success. In three months, Il Trovatore will be sung, whistled, and played all over Italy!"

ETHAN MORDDEN—OPERA ANECDOTES

WHAT DO YOU THINK OF THIS?

Q How do REAL people get started listening to Opera?

A They focus on **SINGERS**.

Q But but but...Opera singers are so different than...normal singers?

<u>Not</u> as different as you think.

Opera has a lot in common with the music you already listen to. Many popular singers have "Operatic" styles.

**Like:** Any singer who really belts a song out (LaBelle, Aretha, Streisand, Liza Minelli).

Like: Any singer who lives off high notes (Mariah Carey, Streisand, Tony Williams [Platters], the "Everybody-dance-now!" lady).

**Like:** Any singer who sings with "excessive" emotional intensity (Roy Orbison, Michael Bolton, Judy Garland).

Whitney Huston would make a hell of an Opera singer: She sings high and low, with resonance and soul

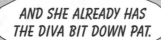
AND SHE ALREADY HAS THE DIVA BIT DOWN PAT.

All the Italian stallions from Al Martino to Tony Bennet were damn near Opera singers; ditto for Soul studs like Jackie Wilson (the R&B Caruso) and Jazz coloraturas like Sarah Vaughn, Have you ever noticed that Johnny Cash and John Lee Hooker both have beautiful bass voices?

Speaking of Similarities

The honesty, intimacy, and incredible warmth in Gladys Knight's voice are exactly the qualities that made Caruso such a popular singer. The similarity in singing styles between specific Opera Zingers and Real singers (e.g. Smokey Robinson/Benjamino Gigli) might even be a good place for a new listener to start.

Billie Holiday and Maria Callas are two of a kind in a way that transcends music, from their breathtaking musical intelligence to their self-negating private lives (at the risk of sounding completely nuts, I believe that there was some kind of spiritual bond between those two brilliant black and white Athenas).

Satchmo's hanky and Pavarotti's hanky? Damned if I know. (Jung's Theory of Parallel Hankies?) The Lord worketh in mysterious ways, Grasshopper.

But check this out:

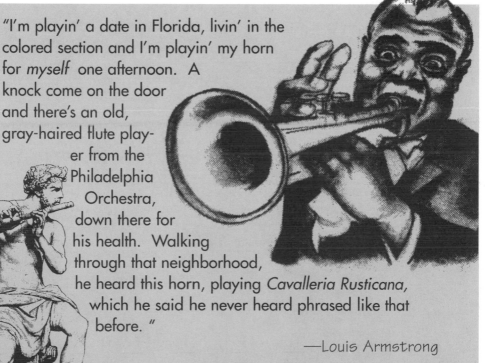

"I'm playin' a date in Florida, livin' in the colored section and I'm playin' my horn for *myself* one afternoon. A knock come on the door and there's an old, gray-haired flute player from the Philadelphia Orchestra, down there for his health. Walking through that neighborhood, he heard this horn, playing *Cavalleria Rusticana*, which he said he never heard phrased like that before."

—Louis Armstrong

Did You Know, Yo...?

Pop singers often record Opera arias:

★ Della Reese's hit, "Don't You Know" is Musetta's waltz from Puccini's <u>La Boheme</u>;

★ Jackie Wilson's big recording of "Night" is Delilah's aria from Saint Saens' <u>Samson</u> <u>and</u> <u>Delilah</u>;

★ Big voiced crooners Tony Martin and Alan Dale sang arias from *Pagliacci*;

★ Linda Ronstadt tried both Opera and Operetta;

★ Johnny Mathis sang at the San Francisco Opera Company;

★ Streisand recorded an album of classical songs, but instead of singing Opera arias where that resonant voice of hers belonged, she sang tasteful, boring "art songs."

WHO KNOWS? MAYBE SHE TRIED "UN BEL DI" AND COULDN'T CUT IT?

To make the jump from *normal* singers to OperaZingers, all you need is something to ignite a little Spark.

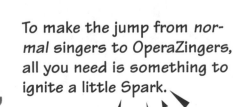

How Do I IGNITE the SPARK?

It's usually a singer that ignites the spark, but it could be a melody from a movie or TV (like the two-woman duets from <u>Tales of Hoffmann</u>, <u>Madame Butterfly</u>, and <u>Lakme</u>). Athletes are attracted to Opera, partly because of the strength and skill involved, and partly because athletes have heroic dreams.

> OPERA IS HERO MUSIC.

If you've lost your dreams, Opera is a good place to get them back.

Ethnicity and Well-Padded Role Models

Seeing yourself in one of the performers can ignite the spark.

If you're not exactlly the skinny type, it's kind of wonderful to see all those well-padded people being admircd and adored:

> SPARK!

If you are seriously ethnic (or, god forbid, a minority), seeing someone from your ethnic group loved, admired, respected, can light your fire...

Paul Robeson, born in Princeton, N.J. in 1898, was an honors student at Rutgers University, twice made the All America Football Team, graduated from Columbia Law School, worked in a New York law firm, played in an N.F.L. Championship football game, was a professional stage actor, and a fine Opera and concert singer—a bass. In 1928 he moved to England, then returned to sing a sold-out concert at Carnegie Hall. He specialized in black folk music and songs from Italian and German Opera and he spoke 20 languages. In 1934, he visited the Soviet Union. In 1948, he attended the World Peace Congress. In 1959, he gave his final performance of <u>Othello</u>. He died in 1976. He often said, **"I must feed the people with my songs."**

> Spark, hell! Robeson lived a life so full it could ignite a BOMB!

> I DON'T WEAR A HAT, SO I TAKE MY HEAD OFF TO YOU, MR. ROBESON.

MEANWHILE, BACK AT THE OPERA HOUSE...

111

ETHNIC DIVERSITY

Major Opera houses are like ethnic Noah's arks: They have a couple of everything. It's not unusual to see an Opera featuring a Spanish tenor, an African American soprano, a Polish mezzo, a Puerto Rican baritone, a bass from Nebraska, and a Jewish conductor. The Metropolitan Opera roster includes Japanese, Chinese and Korean singers who specialize in Italian opera!

Other things can ignite the Spark: Movies or boredom or the irrepressible impulse to capitalize words like Passion, Romance, Destiny, even though in Real Life they're extremely lower-case.

But make no mistake about it—80% of the time, the Spark is lit by a Singer. An Opera singer. It starts with one particular singer.

All you have to do is find him, her, it, or them.

A List of Miraculous Singers

...and Stefan's List

If I had to name three singers who would be most likely to Bliss you out, have you kissing snakes on the forehead, and send shivers up your spine, I'd say **Jussi Bjoerling**, **Leontyne Price**, and the young **Ezio Pinza**.

Jussi Bjoerling

Bjoerling is the guy who "introduced" me to Opera. It went like this: I was in the Army, a 19-year-old rhythm & blues Detroit kid, all libido and no brains, sentenced to six months in Alabama, when one day a friend I didn't particularly like came up to me, drunk as an upright man can be, and, in a tone you'd use to confess that you molested nuns, whispered, "I'm studying Opera." He begged me to listen to a record with him—"I have to share this with somebody." Even at 19, I was supportive of friends, even if I didn't particularly like them, so I tried (pretended?) to be broad minded. He put on the record; I sat in a dark corner so he couldn't read my face; he said it was a guy named Jussi Bjoerling; he thanked me; he sat down; he shut up.

BAM! BONK! BOINK!

I'm not a very holy guy—I've never had a certifiable religious experience—but, at 19, that was as close as I'd come. I had never heard anything so miraculous in my life. Clarity, Power, Beauty, Focus. There was no getting used to it, no studying books or librettos, no intention to "appreciate" anything (I was a teenager—I already <u>knew</u> everything). In a flash, like Saint What's-his-name getting knocked off his pony, I was an instant convert. One of Plato's most off-the-wall ideas is that we have the knowledge of nearly everything already inside us; all we need is a dude like Socrates to ask us the right questions or a drunk to play a record that will teach us what we already know...

There was no learning, no transition, no anything! I heard the Voice, and BAM! It was as if there was a door locked inside of me that I was unaware of, and this, *Voice*, unlocks it.

The door opens; I open; everything opens.

I am not the person I was.

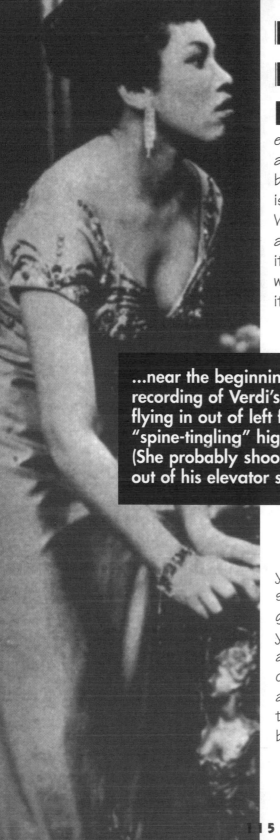

Leontyne Price

If I had to choose the single most electrifying voice I'd ever heard on anybody, anywhere, ever, it would be the Voice of Leontyne Price. It is as rich, opulent, thrilling—if any Voice could slap you in the head and throw you up against the wall, it would be Leontyne's. (I don't want to get too carried away or it'll sound like she's paying me.)

...near the beginning of the Price/Bergonzi recording of Verdi's <u>Ernani</u>, Leontyne comes flying in out of left field with the most "spine-tingling" high note you ever heard! (She probably shook Carlo Bergonzi right out of his elevator shoes!)

With both Bjoerling and Price, you'll find a range of recordings some 30 years apart. My suggestion: Get 'em young—the younger the better. At a later age, both singers will have developed more finesse, but finesse is a bridesmaid's art. I want you to hear the the Voice in all its beautiful brainless glory.

Ezio Pinza

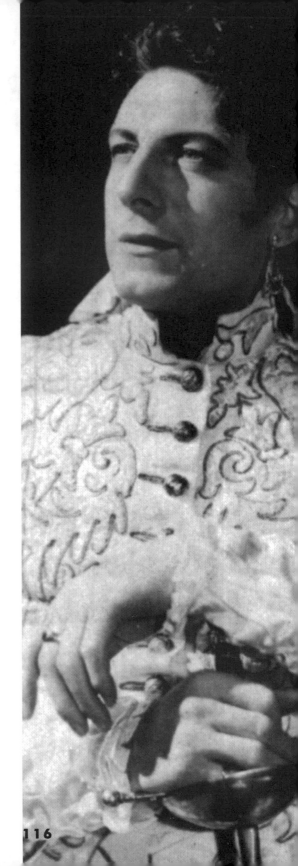

After not hearing the young Pinza for a couple months, I'll put on one of his recordings from the 1930s...in one of my minds, I stagger backward, I clutch my chest, I mutter, "I'm coming, Elizabeth." Pinza's voice is so magnificent that it's hard to hold in the mind—truly one of the Voices of God.

However: Pinza's voice had a "window" of magnificence: In his early years (the 1920s), he had such a fast vibrato that it tended to obscure the beauty of his voice. In later years (after 1940), his voice sounded much more common (merely very very good instead of miraculous).

I guarandamnedtee you, if you listen to a recording of Pinza from the 1930s, you will know why people like me turn into sanctified maniacs over Opera.

After Bjoerling, Price, and Pinza, which singers are most likely to grab you by the ears and demand your attention? I will defer to Stefan's list.

Stefan's List

Stefan Zucker is the man who writes, edits, publishes, organizes, broadcasts, eats, sleeps, and dreams about <u>Opera Fanatic</u> magazine and radio show. He knows and loves singing as much as any fanatic on earth. He is the most democratic fanatic I've ever come across. Although he is obsessively devoted to singers like Magda Olivero, he encourages and celebrates different opinions. If you phone into his radio show, he treats your opinion with great respect, even if you don't know Opera from toothpaste.

Stefan compiles a list of Listeners' Favorite Singers.

With no further delay, here is Stefan's List.

Stephan Zucker's Listeners' Favorite Singers

FAVORITE FEMALE SINGER OF THE PAST
1. Maria Callas
2. Rosa Ponselle
3. Magda Olivero
4. Claudia Muzio
5. Zinka Milanov &
5. Renata Tebaldi (tie)
7. Kirsten Flagstad
8. Conchita Supervia
9. Amelita Galli-Curci &
9. Lily Pons (tie)

FAVORITE FEMALE SINGER OF THE 1980s
1. Monserrat Caballe
2. Magda Olivero
3. Mirela Freni
4. Joan Sutherland
5. Jessye Norman
6. Renata Scotto
7. Leontyne Price
8. Victoria De Los Angeles
9. Birgit Nilsson
10. Eva Marton

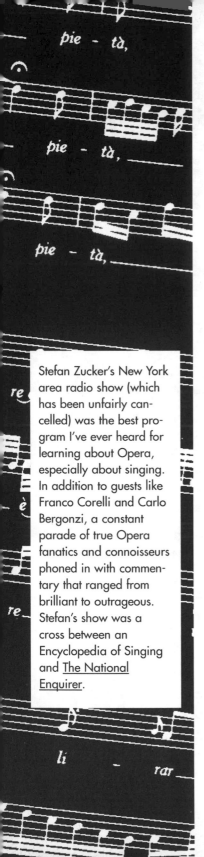

Stefan Zucker's New York area radio show (which has been unfairly cancelled) was the best program I've ever heard for learning about Opera, especially about singing. In addition to guests like Franco Corelli and Carlo Bergonzi, a constant parade of true Opera fanatics and connoisseurs phoned in with commentary that ranged from brilliant to outrageous. Stefan's show was a cross between an Encyclopedia of Singing and The National Enquirer.

When it comes to Stefan's listeners' Favorite Tenors, the list is shorter and less definite, but it always starts with Four Tenors (catchy title): 1. **Franco Corelli;** 2. **Jussi Bjoerling;** 3. **Enrico Caruso;** 4. **Benjamino Gigli.**

A word about Stefan's listerns' lists

Magda Olivero places second on one list and third on the other. That's a bit unusual; many Opera listeners have never heard of Olivero, and those who have generally wouldn't list her in the top 20 singers. But those who like her, **love** her; she is, I think, an ideal choice for an Opera Fanatic's favorite singer.

Franco Corelli, on the other hand, is an odd choice to place high on Stefan's list, partly because he was so popular. (No self-respecting Fanatic has the same favorites as The Masses!) Corelli was a handsome dude with big high notes.

Stefan's personal all-time favorites

Francesco Tamagno (tenor), **Magda Olivero** (soprano), **Irene Minghini-Cattaneo** (mezzo), **Giovanni Martinelli** (tenor), **Maria Farneti** & **Ester Mazzoleni** (sopranos).

Zucker isn't alone in his admiration of Tamagno. J. B. STEANE (**VOICES: Singers & Critics**) writes: "I have just taken down three of his records: it is an amazing sound, coming through from 1903 with massive power and absolute clarity."

Snoop through Opera's past—it's a goldmine of spectacular singers. Stephan Zucker even puts out an **Opera Fanatic's Catalogue**, featuring hard-to-get videos, tapes, Cds. (See the Section on Resources for the address.)

DAVID'S FAVORITE SINGERS

(Ital./Ger. doesn't refer to the singer but to the operas he/she sang.)

A Few of Ron ITALIAN TENORS (Currently active Singers are <u>Underlined</u>)

◆ **Caruso:** My nominee for the most outrageously beautiful two minutes of singing by anyone, ever, is Brother Caruso's singing in *"Dormi pur"* (Flotow's MARTA).

◆ Two wonderfully overcooked (and deceased) Tenors I'm currently enjoying like a maniac are Mario (Iron Lungs) **Del Monaco** and Benjamino (Phony Baloney) **Gigli**.

◆ **Giuseppe di Stefano, Antonio Cortis, Jose Luccione, Giacomo Lauri-Volpi**

◆ The line on **<u>Pavarotti</u>** and **<u>Domingo</u>** is that Pavarotti has the more beautiful "instrument," but Domingo is the more accomplished singer. I agree, but make no mistake: Domingo has a voice of great beauty; it's just that Pavarotti may have THE <u>most</u> <u>beautiful</u> voice of any Tenor ever. (Pavarotti and Pinza, in their prime, are the only two voices my mind can't hold; their beauty exceeds my memory.)

◆ **<u>Neil Schicoff</u>, <u>Dano Raffanti</u>,** & **<u>Alan Glassman</u>** are fine tenors.

◆ **<u>Giuseppe Moreno</u>** has an old time vibrato and a soul to match. (Thanks, Stefan)

GERMAN TENORS

◆ Lauritz **Melchoir** is one hell of a Heldentenor: a huge, ringing, passionate voice.

◆ Unique Tenors: **Richard Tauber, Marcel Wittrisch, Helge Roswaenge, <u>Reiner Goldberg</u>**

◆ Lyric Tenors: **Josef Schmidt, Fritz Wunderlich, <u>Siegfried Jerusalem</u>,**

BASSES & BARITONES

◆ Baritones **Tito Gobbi** and **<u>Giorgio Zacanaro</u>**.

◆ *BORIS CHRISTOF:* magnificent as *BORIS GUDONOV* (Mussorgsky) and **<u>DON CARLOS</u>** (Verdi).

◆ **<u>Kurt Moll</u>**, a Bass with a truly beautiful voice, is untouchable in Mozart's *ABDUCTION FROM THE SERAGLIO* and Wagner's *PARSIFAL* (two very different roles).

◆ **<u>Samuel Ramey</u>** slithers around like a dancer, goes shirtless in every Opera, has one of the finest Bass voices, and he can sing florid Rossini or Handel arias.

◆ **<u>James Morris</u>**, the "other" American Bass, didn't knock me out until he started singing the role of Wotan (in Wagner's *RING*). Now he's The Man.

ITALIAN SOPRANOS & MEZZOS
◆ **Conchita Supervia** with her radical vibrato & **Claudia Muzio**, a Dramatic Soprano.
◆ **Maria Callas** was one intense lady. The aria that first got me crazy for her was *"Suicidio"* (Giordano's LA GIOCONDA). Scope out the Opera MEDEA (Cherubini).
◆ **Tebaldi** had a big ringing voice; she & Del Monaco own FANCIULLA DEL WEST (Puccini).
◆ **Sutherland** is amazing, especially when she's paired with Pavarotti or Horne.
◆ <u>Marilyn Horne</u> may be the most phenomenal singer alive. Her downshift from ringing high notes to deep rumbling. chest-voice is liable to knock your hat off!
◆ <u>Rosalind Plowright, Renee Fleming</u>

GERMAN SOPRANOS & MEZZOS
◆ **Frida Leider, Lotte Lehman, Elizabeth Schwarzkopf, Kirsten Flagstad**
◆ **Birgit Nilsson** had a *huge* ringing voice that asserted itself over any orchestra.
◆ **Ljuba Welitsch**: Her recording of the final scene of Strauss' *Salome* is inspired.
◆ **Gundula Janowicz** singing Strauss' FOUR LAST SONGS is like the opening of a flower.
◆ Most voices *enter* you; <u>**Jessye Norman's**</u> envelops you in great waves of sound.

STUFF
◆ Miraculous recordings of live Met broadcasts of the 1930s and 40s feature **Pinza, Gigli**, and **Elizabeth Rethberg**—all three of them, voices kissed by God. Ms. Rethberg sounds like she's going to jump right off the record into your lap.
◆ French soprano **Mado Robin** is Opera's Queen of the High Notes. Truly amazing.
◆ Two singers with voices that are beautiful in a "normal" non-Operatic way are <u>**Fredericka von Stade**</u> and <u>**Kathleen Battle**</u>.

NEWCOMERS TO WATCH
◆ Coloratura mezzo, <u>**Cecilia Bartoli**</u>, especially when she sings Rossini
◆ Bass-Baritone, <u>**Bryn Terfel**</u>, especially if he sings the role of Wotan.
◆ Bel Canto Tenor, <u>**Raul Jiminez**</u>
◆ German Tenor, <u>**Peter Seifert**</u>
◆ Baritone <u>**Vladimir Chernov,**</u>

LISTENING to WAGNER

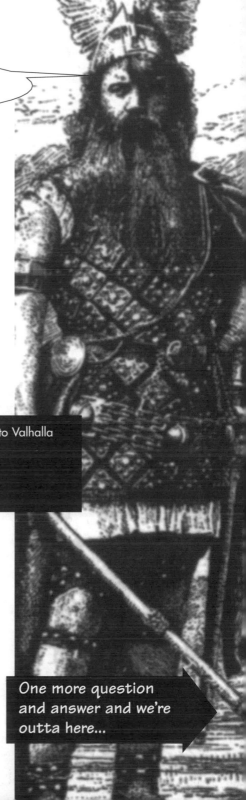

Many people are intimidated by Wagner.

HE'D LOVE THAT!

Q: Is there a painless way to get started listening to his music?

A: Yes, but it's different than with other composers. With other Opera composers, you find your way in through *singers*. With Wagner, you find your way in through his <u>orchestral</u> music. Pick up one of those tapes/records/CDs with names like "Orchestral Selections from Wagner's Ring." If there's nothing on there that grabs your attention...call a doctor. A few of the obvious choices are:

- ◆ The Entrance of the Gods into Valhalla
- ◆ The Ride of the Valkyries
- ◆ Siegfried's Rhine Journey
- ◆ Siegfried's Funeral March

Don't even think of saying you don't like Wagner. (I'll jump off this page and come upside your head!) There's such variety in his music that, if you don't like one piece, you're bound to love another.

And if that doesn't work—or even if it does—there is a hilarious and educational monologue by Anna Russell, a British lady, on Wagner's Ring. It's brilliant.

One more question and answer and we're outta here...

121

GodSong

Q   Why are there so many good-to-great African American female Opera singers? Price, Arroyo, Mitchel, Verrett, Bumbry, Norman, Battle, Hendricks, Alexander, Blackwell...to name a few.

WHY?

A   Because (this is an opinion, not a fact) of the profound similarity between Opera and Gospel singing. African American women make great Opera singers because they, more than any of us, are used to singing directly to God.   That, my babies, is what Opera at its best is all about.

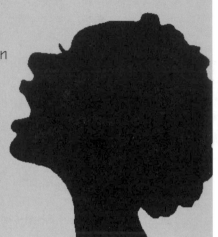

NOW I'LL TAKE YOU TO THE *Opera...*

ACT FOUR: 30 Operas

Title	Composer	Language	Year	Style
AIDA	Verdi	Italian	1871	Late Verdi
BARBER OF SEVILLE	Rossini	Italian	1816	Bel Canto—comic
BLUEBEARD'S CASTLE	Bartok	Hungarian	1918	Modern Allegorical
LA BOHEME	Puccini	Italian	1896	Romantic/Verismo
BORIS GODUNOV	Mussorgsky	Russian	1874	Russian Historical
CARMEN	Bizet	French	1875	French Verismo
CAVALLERIA RUSTICANA	Mascagni	Italian	1890	Italian Verismo
DON GIOVANNI	Mozart	Ital.(Ger.)	1787	Opera Buffa
ELIXIR OF LOVE	Donizetti	Italian	1832	Bel Canto—comic
FAUST	Gounod	French	1859	French Romantic
FLEDERMAUS	Strauss, J.	German	1874	German Operetta
LES HUGUENOTS	Meyerbeer	French	1836	French Grand Opera
LUCIA DI LAMMERMOOR	Donizetti	Italian	1835	Bel Canto—serious
MADAM BUTTERFLY	Puccini	Italian	1904	Romantic/Verismo
MAGIC FLUTE	Mozart	German	1791	German Singspeil
MANON	Massenet	French	1884	French Romantic
NORMA	Bellini	Italian	1831	Bel Canto—serious
PAGLIACCI	Leoncavallo	Italian	1892	Italian Verismo
PETER GRIMES	Britten	British	1945	Modern British
PORGY & BESS	Gershwin	American	1935	Modern American
RIGOLETTO	Verdi	Italian	1851	Early Verdi
ROSENKAVALIER	Strauss, R.	German	1911	NeoClassic Parody
TALES OF HOFFMANN	Offenbach	French	1881	Romantic Allegory
TOSCA	Puccini	Italian	1900	Romantic/Verismo
LA TRAVIATA	Verdi	Italian	1853	Middle Verdi
IL TROVATORE	Verdi	Italian	1853	Middle Verdi
RHEINGOLD	Wagner	German	1869	The Ring Cycle, 1
DIE WALKURE	Wagner	German	1870	The Ring Cycle, 2
SIEGFRIED	Wagner	German	1876	The Ring Cycle, 3
GOTTERDAMMERUNG	Wagner	German	1876	The Ring Cycle, 4

TWO QUESTIONS

Q How can I understand Opera if I don't understand the language it's sung in?

A A few years ago, on a moonlit night in Central Park, my wife and I saw classical actress Gloria Foster play Clytemnestra in the ol' Greek drama <u>Agamemnon</u>. Foster was awesome. In the climactic scene, she didn't use a word of English or any other dictionary language. She used her body and her soul and syllables and sounds and she conveyed the most profound sense of anguish I've ever seen outside of real life. You couldn't misunderstand it even if you wanted to.

Point 1: *Trust yourself—go with your feelings—you'll understand.*

Point 2: Most Opera plots make better sense if you don't understand the language. Like the man says...

"Opera in English is...just about as sensible as baseball in Italian."
H.L. MENCHEN
[1880-1956]

> I am ravished by opera, on condition that I have only a vague idea of what it is about.
> JAMES AGATE [1877-1947]

Point 3: I've made the assumption here that you aren't going to rush out and learn Italian, German, etc.; if Opera does entice you to learn a language or two, you can thank me later.

On what basis did you choose the Operas? The most listener friendly? The most popular? Most important? Personal favorites?

If I chose the <u>most</u> <u>popular</u> Operas, you'd have two French Operas (<u>Carmen</u> and <u>Faust</u>), one German (<u>Magic</u> <u>Flute</u>), and the rest Italian (<u>Cav</u> & <u>Pag</u>, a few Bel Canto Operas, and everything ever written by Verdi and Puccini).

If I chose <u>my</u> <u>favorites</u>, we'd have a Rossini festival, lots of Bellini and Donizetti, a couple French tear-jerkers (<u>Werther</u>, <u>Romeo</u> & <u>Juliet</u>), a few oddities (Respighi's <u>La</u> <u>Fiamma</u>, Strauss' <u>Guntram</u>), a drastically condensed version of Wagner's Ring (except for <u>Die</u> <u>Walkure</u>, which we love in its entirety) and we'd omit <u>Porgy</u>, <u>Carmen</u>, and probably <u>Don</u> <u>Giovanni</u>, and trade the Verdi, Puccini, and Strauss Operas in for their less famous counterparts (<u>Salome</u>, <u>Girl</u> <u>of</u> <u>the</u> <u>Golden</u> <u>West</u>, <u>Manon</u> <u>Lescault</u>, <u>La</u> <u>Forza</u> <u>del</u> <u>destino</u>, <u>Don</u> <u>Carlos</u>, <u>Sicilian</u> <u>Vespers</u>.)

If I chose the <u>most</u> <u>important</u>, we'd have snorers like Gluck and Schoenberg, more Wagner, Monteverdi, Beethoven's <u>Fidelio</u>.

I Chose the Operas Based on These Criteria:

1 First and foremost, they had to be listener-friendly—something you could really dig listening to.

2 The second criterion: That they had to be as varied as possible, both linguistically and stylistically. They cover seven different languages (as any fool knows, English is one language, American is another). Stylistically, they cover high and low Mozart, funny and serious Bel Canto, a 20-year span of Verdi, French and Italian verismo, French Grand Opera, Russian Opera, French Tear Jerker, German Operetta, French Operetta gone highbrow, Hungarian allegorical Opera, German neo-classical, modern British, Jazzified American, Puccini and Wagner—each a class unto himself.

3 Wagner's Ring Cycle had to get in.

4 When I had any wiggle-room, I chose the ones I loved.

HERE THEY ARE (I HOPE YOU LOVE 'EM)...

126

 AIDA

Giuseppe Verdi

Act 1:

Radames wants to become a General in the Egyptian Army and marry Aida—but Amneris, the Egyptian King's daughter, is hot for Radames' body.

Act 2:

Radames and the Egyptian Army return triumphantly from war...with Aida's father (the King of Ethiopia) in captivity.

Act 3:

Aida sweettalks Radames into betraying the Egyptian Army. Radames does it, then overcome by guilt, he surrenders to the Egyptian priests.

Act 4:

The priests punish Radames by burying him alive in a tomb. Princess Amneris weeps melodically at the tomb's entrance. Aida, who has been hiding voluptuously in the tomb, reveals herself to Radames so they sing a love duet...and die together.

Barber of Seville

Giocchino Rossini

Act 1:

Count Almaviva serenades Rosina, but her guardian Dr. Bartolo, won't let her see Almaviva because the old lech Bartolo wants her for himself.

The Barber and the Count hatch a plot whereby the Count disguises himself as a drunk soldier assigned to live in Dr. Bartolo's house. Disruption ensues and the coppers arrive.

Act 2:

The Count comes to Bartolo's house newly disguised as a Professor to sit in for Rosina's "sick" music teacher.

The Count, with the Barber's help, overcomes all the bad guys and marries Rosina.

COMPARE: Giovanni Paisello (1740-1816) wrote an earlier version of *The Barber of Seville* (1782).

BLUEBEARD'S CASTLE
Bela Bartok

Act 1:

Bluebeard, a cross between Don Juan and Dracula, "interviews" Judith to see if she'll become his wife. He points to seven doors flanking the hall of his castle. Through the first door, a torture chamber is revealed. The second door is hung with Bluebeard's weaponry. One by one the doors are opened, each worse than than the one before. ("Sorrow, Judith. Sorrow," is the way Bluebeard describes his Lake of Tears.) Bluebeard opens the last locked door only after Judith's insistence. One by one, Bluebeard's wives file out, "Living, living..." Judith says incredulously. Then she joins Bluebeard's parade of living-dead wives...

"Similar stories appear in European, African, and Eastern folklore; the essentials are [the murderous husband,] the locked and forbidden room, the wife's curiousity... ."
ENCYCLOPEDIA BRITANNICA

It's a one act Opera with two characters. Balsy, experimental, and wonderful. It has such a strong musical identity, that if you hear two chords, you know it's <u>Bluebeard's Castle</u>.

Bottom Line:
Poor struggling artists — "Bohemians" — in 1800s Paris fall madly, melodically in love.

La Boheme

Giacomo Puccini

Act 1:

Rodolfo the poet, Marcello the painter, Colline the philosopher, and Schaunard the musician outslick their landlord, who has come to collect the rent. Roldofo the poet meets Mimi the seamstress and they fall head over heels.

Act 2:

At the cafe Momus, Marcello the painter sees his old girlfriend, Musetta the tart, who sings a famous waltz and sends him on a jive errand.

Act 3:

Outside an inn on the outskirts of Paris, Rodolfo and Mimi decide they can't hack it together and, in an outpouring of melody, break up.

Act 4:

Mimi is dying: Musetta, the tart with the heart of gold, sells her earrings to buy medicine; Rodolfo shows up just past the nick of time; Mimi melodically bites the dust. Rodolfo (Caruso, Gigli, Bjorling, di Stefano, Pavarotti, Domingo) screams her name—"Mimi! Mimi!"—and, even if you're laughing, sends chills through you.

COMPARE:
Leoncavallo (composer of Pagliacci) also wrote a decent version of La Boheme.

BORIS GODUNOV
Modest Mussorgsky

Prologue:

When the Russian Czar Ivan the Terrible died in 1584, one of his sons was a child and the other was a teenage halfwit, so Boris Godunov, the Czar's adviser, became acting Czar. The small child, Dimitri, died in a monastery and the feeble-minded brother died not long after. In *Scene 2*, Boris, the newly crowned Czar, is having trouble with his conscience because he ordered the murder of the little boy.

Act 1:

Five years later, an opportunistic novice monk, who is the same age the dead Dimitri would have been, decides to pretend that he himself is Prince Dimitri.

Act 2:

Boris, in a great monologue, laments that things are going badly in Russia and everyone blames the Czar. His advisor Prince Shuiski warns Boris that a pretender after the throne is winning the people to his side. Boris asks Shuiski if he's certain that it was little Dimitri who was killed. Shuiski leaves; Boris imagines that he sees the bloodstained body of the murdered boy and begs God for forgiveness.

Act 3 & 4:

The false Dimitri promises to rid the people of Boris; they follow him.

An old monk tells Boris of a shepherd's dream about the murder of Dimitri. Boris, gasping for air, sends for his son Feodor. Boris sings an incredibly moving farewell to little Feodor, then dies gloriously.

JEEZ, DAD...
CHILL OUT, WILL YA?...

Carmen

Georges Bizet

Bottom Line: A love story between a sexy, manipulative Gypsy girl (Carmen) and a naive solder (Don Jose) who's just dyin' to be made a fool of.

HOLY SMOKES, DON JOSÉ...WHAT DID SHE SAY TO YOU?...

Act 1:

In Spain: Don José arrests Carmen for causing a disturbance. She gives him a big smile and a little feel and he lets her escape...for which he is arrested.

Act 2:

At an inn: Carmen meets the disgraced José after he is released from jail, gives him a big smile and a little feel, and talks him into joining her band of smugglers.

Act 3:

Meanwhile: Micaela, Don José's old squeeze, comes looking for him to tell him that his mother is dying. Don Jose goes to see his dying mother...

Act 4:

Meanwhile: Carmen becomes the lover of a bullfighter (probably just to shut him up so he'll stop singing that damned *"Toreador"* song). Jealous Don José—no big surprise—loses his cool, sings some dynamite high notes, and kills Carmen.

CAVALLERIA RUSTICANA

Pietro Mascagni

Act 1:

Easter Sunday, Town Square, Sicily: Santuzza— the nice girl—is worried that her hotblooded fiance Turiddu is having an affair with the hotblooded Lola who was once Turiddu's ol' lady but is now married to Alfio the hotblooded

TURIDDU IS DEFINITELY HAVING AN AFFAIR, BUT WITH WHOM, LOLA, WITH WHOM?

GULP!

Teamster. (Sicily? Alfio the Teamster? You could finish the damn thing yourself!)

I DON'T THINK THAT'S THE RESPONSE SHE WAS HOPING FOR...

Outside the church: Santuzza tries crying to Mamma Lucia (Turiddu's mother—a saint), but Mamma doesn't want to hear it.

Santuzza goes whining to Turiddu, appealing to his sense of fair play and justice. Turiddu knocks her to the ground. Santuzza, really pissed now, tells Lola's husband, Alfio the Teamster. ("MaaRONE!)

Alfio the Teamster challenges Turiddu to a duel. Turiddu gets drunk and barely finishes singing goodbye to his hotblooded mother before Alfio the hotblooded Teamster kills him.

DON GIOVANNI

Wolfgang A. Mozart

Act 1:

With the help of his servant Leporello, Don puts a move on Anna, kills her father, gets away from her boyfriend Ottavio, runs into an old girlfriend (Elvira), and leaves Leporello behind to "explain." Don runs across a pretty young thang (Zerlina) and invites her to his castle. Act I ends as Zerlina runs screaming in pantyhose terror and the Don is cornered by all of his enemies at once. Don may be a lech, but he's no coward: He swashbuckles his way to freedom.

Act 2:

The randy Don trades clothes with Leporello with the intent of hitting on Elvira's maid but ends up outsmarting himself: Elvira sees Leporello dressed in the Don's clothing, and runs off with Leporello. (Mozart wrote a "low comedy" scene that comes next, but most Opera productions omit it because it doesn't fit in with Mozart's lofty reputation.) As a joke, Don invites a statue of Anna's dead father to dinner. The statue actually comes, and Don and his palace disappear in flames. Sometimes the Opera ends there; sometimes it ends the way Mozart wrote it: with a goofy finale in which everyone tells us their plans—both young couples with be married, Leporello finds a nice dull master, and Elvira enters a convent. (Maybe that's why Pope What's-His-Name had that Opera house burned down; maybe he got sick of all those deranged Opera ladies running off to convents?)

PARDON ME FOR ASKING, BUT ARE YOU STONED?

Elixr of Love

Gaetano Donizetti

Act 1:

Adina, a rich chick, is loved, admired, and lusted after by both Sergeant Belcore and Nemorino, a shy but dumb peasant. Nemorino is conned by Dr. Dulcamara the "medicine man" (in a duet as full of surprise and life as a magician's hat) into spending all of his money for a Love Potion (wine) that is *guaranteed* to make Adina love him within 24 hours. Unfortunately, Adina promises to marry Sergeant Belcore that night.

I CAN'T KEEP THE BABES OFF ME!

SO, ARE YOU SURE THIS STUFF WILL WORK FOR ME?

Act 2:

Nemorino, no dummy, comes up with a brilliant solution: He joins the friggin Army and uses his enlistment money to buy a Magic Potion (wine) that is *guaranteed* to work in a half-hour. After he gets a little bombed, Nemorino (Caruso, Gigli, Bjorling, Pavarotti, and every tenor in the universe) sings "*Una furtiva lagrima...*". Adina falls madly in love with him, buys back his enlistment, and they...be doop, be doop, be doop.

SOLD

135

FAUST

Charles Gounod

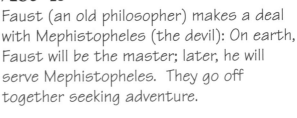

ARE YOU BOARD CERTIFIED?

Act 1:

Faust (an old philosopher) makes a deal with Mephistopheles (the devil): On earth, Faust will be the master; later, he will serve Mephistopheles. They go off together seeking adventure.

Act 2:

Faust, young and handsome, romances Marguerite. (He romances her so well that she becomes pregnant.)

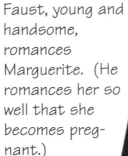

OOH, FAUST, YOU DEVIL!

Act 3:

In church: Marguerite prays that her sins be pardoned. Her brother Valentine comes back from the war to avenge his sister's honor, sings one of the prettiest baritone arias in Grand Opry...then gets killed by Faust.

Act 4:

Marguerite is in prison for killing her child. She prays to God—God saves her. You're right: The story _does_ sound unfinished. That's where the music comes in: The _music_ finishes it. The music sends Marguerite, Faust, you, me, your old Volkswagen—all of us—straight up to...give it whatever name you like.

COMPARE: Arrigio Boito (1842-1918), author of some of Verdi's best librettos, composed _Mephistophele_ (1868), an Opera that is as good or better than Mr. Gounoud's _Faust_.

136

Die Fledermaus

Johann Strauss

> "...Beverly Sills, who can sing everything from Verdi ballads to Strauss operations."
>
> President Gerald Ford, Introducing opera singer Beverly Sills at the White House, 1975

As usual, the Prez got his verbals mixeds up: The word he wanted was "Operetta." (Operetta = Spoken dialogue with arias, sometimes beautiful, sometimes so pretty it's disgusting; it <u>always</u> has a happy ending.) The Strauss in question isn't *Richard*, it's *Johann*, the heavyweight champ of the welterweight art of German Operetta. This one is so good that the Met features it on New Year's Eve.

WOULD YA LIKE TO BUY A WATCH?

Act 1:

Alfredo, a former boyfriend—and an Italian tenor—serenades Rosalinda, Eisenstein's wife. Eisenstein is supposed to go to jail that night but he goes to a party. He'll go to jail tomorrow.

Act 2:

The party is a masked ball thrown by Prince Orlofsky. Eisenstein doesn't recognize his wife, who flirts with him and takes his watch.

Act 3:

Eisenstein reports to jail the next morning, but he finds that Alfredo, who'd been at Eisenstein's house sniffing after Rosalinda, was mistaken for Eisenstein and taken to jail in his stead. (What it lacks in dramatic urgency, it makes up for in toe-tapping music.)

137

Les Huguenots

Giacomo Meyerbeer

Prelude & Acts 1, 2, 3, 4, (and sometimes) 5:

The growing hostility between Catholics and Protestants (Huguenots) in 16th century France impels Queen Marguerite to find some way to unite them. To that end, she asks Raoul, a young Huguenot nobleman, to marry Valentina, the daughter of a prominent Catholic.

When Valentina shows herself, Raoul furiously backs out of the deal to marry her—because he's been led to believe that she's the mistress of his Catholic friend, Count de Nevers. By the time Raoul admits to himself that he's hoplessly crazy about Valentina, she's been promised to de Nevers (although she is madly in love with Raoul and has even saved his life).

Raoul, brain dead with love, sneaks into Valentina's room. to "bid her a final farewell," but when he hears her father and other Catholic leaders coming, he hides behind a curtain. To his horror, he hears them planning to massacre the Huguenots that very night, the eve of St. Bartholomew. He goes to warn his friends, but the massacre is already in full swing. Valentina joins him and dies in his arms.

There are lots of great recorded excerpts from Les Huguenots. One of the greatest is a recording of German tenor Marcel Wittrisch and soprano Margarete Teschemacher singing the Raoul/Valentina duet

Lucia di Lammermoor

Gaetano Donizetti

Act 1:

Enrico needs money and wants his sister Lucia to marry rich Arturo in a "marriage of convenience"— Enrico's convenience. Lucia is in love with Edgardo, a guy from the neighborhood (e.g., Caruso, Pavarotti, etc.) who saved her life.

Act 2:

Lucia's slippery brother not only intercepts all the letters Edgardo sends her, but the slimeball even forges a letter saying that Edgardo has married another lady. Lucia, heartbroken, marries the rich cat.

Act 3:

Lucia goes extremely crazy, stumbling around, singing music of impossible fanciness...she kills her husband, then herself. Edgardo, her love-boy, hears about the tragedy, he kills himself.

note: Although this is a juicy role for Sopranos, they sort of hate it because, after they die, the Tenor has the last 15 minutes all to himself.

MADAM BUTTERFLY

Giacomo Puccini

Act 1:

Japan: A marriage broker arranges a union between Lt. Pinkerton and Madam Butterfly (a.k.a. Cio-Cio-San). Sharpless, the American Consul, warns Pinkerton that

he isn't taking the marriage seriously enough. Butterfly's family rejects her for marrying a foreigner.

Act 2:

Japan: Pinkerton has been gone for three years. A Japanese dude wants to marry Butterfly but she tells him she's already married. She has a child, whom she's nicknamed "Trouble."

Act 3:

Japan: Pinkerton returns with his new American wife and learns that he has a son. The grief-stricken Butterfly kills herself.

Bottom Line:
Prince Tamino,
with the help of
his magic flute,
rescues Princess
Pamina.

Magic Flute

Wolfgand A.. Mozart

Act 1:

Prince Tamino is saved
from a bad snake by three
women who hang out with
the Queen of the Night. Papageno, a
bullslinging birdcatcher, takes credit for killing the snake, but the
women punish him for being
a jive turkey.

The Queen of the Night sends Tamino
and Pa-Pa-Pa-Papageno to rescue her daughter
Pamina from Sarastro. The big-hearted Queen
gives Tamino a magic flute and Papageno magic
bells.

Act 2:

Papageno and the
Prince (formerly
known as Tamino)
face a series of
tests from Sarastro.
Tamino ends up with Pamina,
Papageno ends up with a chick who had a face-lift (formerly an old hag) named Papagena, and thunder and
lightning overcome the forces of evil...whoever they
were.

note: Don't fret if you can't tell the Good Guys from the Bad Guys— no one
else can either. (The Prince & Princess are good, so are Papagen<u>O</u> and
Papagen<u>A</u>. Everyone else... damned if I know?

141

 MANON

Jules Massenet

Act 1:

On the way to the convent(!), Manon meets and falls in love with des Grieux. She skips the convent and splits to Paris with des Grieux.

Act 2:

Manon and des Grieux are living happily ever after in Paris until des Grieux is somewhat kidnapped—after which De Bretigny (a filthy rich friend of Manon's slippery brother Lescaut) wins Manon's heart, mind, and body with expensive crap.

Act 3:

Des Grieux is so bummed out he decides to become a priest. Manon finds out, goes and rubs her nice little body up against him; he decides he isn't cut out for the priesthood; they run away together.

Act 4:

They get arrested.

Act 5:

She (you're gonna love this!) is sentenced to be <u>deported to Louisiana</u>—but she dies in des Grieux' arms.

Bottom Line:
A Druid priestess who has sacrificed her honor for the love of a Roman proconsul, learns that he's fallen in love with a younger version.

NORMA

Vincenzo Bellini

Act 1:

Druid high priest Oroveso tells his people that his daughter Norma (the high priestess) will signal them when it's time to revolt against the Roman occupiers.

Act 2:

MY MOM SAID MY BIRTH WAS AN ACCIDENT.

WELL, AT LEAST YOU'RE NOT A VIOLATION OF AN OATH OF CHASTITY...

Unbeknownst to her people, Druid high priestess Norma has violated her oath of chastity and borne two children by Roman Proconsul (Military Governor) Pollione. And if that aint bad enough, Pollione now has the hots for Adalgisa, a younger Druid priestess.

Act 3:

Norma tries to kill her children but she can't. She summons her rival Adalgisa and, after one hell of flashy duet, they become pals again.

Act 4:

Norma heroically decides to be burned to death for her crimes against her people. Pollione, not to be outdone by a mere woman, chooses to die with her. (The resultant outpouring of melody is so eloquent that I'm damn near ready to walk into the fire with them!)

ANYBODY GOT A LIGHT!

Bottom Line: A play-within-a-play within an Opera: An actor finds out that his actress wife is fooling around...so he kills her—in both the Play and Real Life.

I Pagliacci

Ruggiero Leoncavallo

Prologue

Prologue:
Before the curtain goes up, Tonio the clown explains melodically that actors have feelings too, you know...

Act 1:

A troupe of actors arrive: Tonio, a hunchback clown, puts a move on actress Nedda, but he isn't her type, so she rejects him. But local boy Silvio <u>is</u> her type: she agrees to meet him after the performance. Canio, her husband, overhears them. He is furious, heartbroken—but the play must go on—so he sings the most famous aria in Opera: "Vesti la giubba..." "On with the greasepaint..."

NOW THAT'S WHAT I CALL AUDIENCE PARTICIPATION!

Act 2:

The Play: Nedda plays 'Columbine,' Beppe is 'Harlequin,' her back door man, Canio plays 'Pagliacco.' The play is a little too close to real life for the unstable Canio/Pagliacco, so he stabs his wife and her lover.

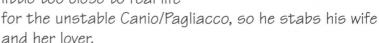

note: I recently saw a TV performance of <u>I Pagliacci</u> with Pavarotti. Luch is no fool: He knows that the voice, though still beautiful, is not what it once was—so for once in his life he decided to act. And it was unbearable! Not because his acting was bad—because it was good. Too good. I saw a jealous maniac killing his wife. Honey, I don't know about you, but that isn't what I do Opera for. Screw realism!

144

Peter Grimes

Benjamin Britten

Prologue:

In a little fishing village in England, fisherman Peter Grimes has lost an apprentice at sea in suspicious circumstances. He is acquitted at the inquest, but warned not to take another apprentice. Only Ellen the schoolmistress, stands behind him.

Act 1:

Balstrode, a retired sea captain, advises Grimes to leave the village and get a fresh start someplace else, but the stubborn Grimes says that he will force the town to respect him by becoming rich. Ellen arrives with a new apprentice for Grimes.

ELLEN, YOU ALWAYS STAND BEHIND ME.

ONLY WHEN THE WIND'S COMING FROM THE BACK.

Act 2:

Sunday, outside the church, Ellen sees bruises on the boy's neck and realizes that Grimes has abused the boy. She quarrels with Grimes, who hits her and storms off, taking the boy to his hut on the cliff top. The villagers take off after him. Grimes hears the mob coming, pushes the boy rudely, and the boy falls to his death.

When the villagers get to Grimes' hut, they see how neat and tidy it is, and decide that a guy that neat can't be so bad, so they go home.

Act 3:

Three days later, Grimes turns up at the village, exhausted. Balstrode tells him that the only way to redeem himself is to sail his boat out to sea and sink it. Grimes does.

Porgy & Bess

George Gershwin

Act 1:

Crown, the local bully, kills a guy at a dice game and leaves town before the coppers can get him. His girl-friend Bess, a little too sexy to be invited in by any of the neighborhood ladies, has no place to live. Porgy, a cripple, lets her stay with him.

Act 2:

Porgy and Bess are happy together. Bess sees Crown at a picnic. Crown, after a month on the run, is most anxious to have a chat with Bess. Bess tries to resist but her spiritual side loses the battle to her hips.

A storm overturns the boat of Jake (a fisherman). Crown and Jake's wife Clara go to help.

Act 3:

Crown returns for Bess, and Porgy strangles him to death. While Porgy is in jail, Sportin' Life (a drug pusher) takes Bess to New York. Porgy, released from jail, follows them on his goat cart.

RIGOLETTO

*Giuseppe
Verdi*

Act 1:

Count Monterone crashes the
Duke of Mantua's party and
denounces the dirty Duke for
"deflowering" Monterone's innocent daughter. The Duke's hunch-
back jester, Rigoletto, makes cruel fun of old
Monterone. The Duke has Monterone arrested, but
before the coppers can take him away, Monterone
puts a "father's curse" on the Duke and Rigoletto.
Rigoletto, himself a father, turns away in terror.

Act 2:

Duke, disguised as a stu-
dent, visits Rig's daugh-
ter Gilda. The Duke's
courtiers (royal groupies)
think that Gilda is
Rigoletto's mistress so, fun guys that they
are, they kidnap her and take her to Duke.

Act 3:

Rig begs for Gilda's release, but the Duke
has deflowered her too.

Act 4:

Rigoletto, good and pissed off, hires an assassin to
ice the Duke. Gilda gets wind of the plan and sacri-
fice her own life for the disgusting Duke. When
Rigoletto discovers that the body in the bag is his
daughter, he screams, *"La maledizione!"*
The friggin <u>curse</u>!

**FREE
GILDA!**

ROSENKAVALIER
Richard Strauss

Act 1:

The Marschallin, a 30-something married woman, realizes that her affair with Octavian, a 17-year-old boy (a "trouser role" sung by a woman), doesn't have much of a future. She sends him to deliver a silver rose (a token of engagement) to beautiful young Sophie...on behalf of her fat old cousin Baron Ochs.

Strauss, to an extent that was unbelievable for a composer of his stature, wrote almost exclusively for women. The most famous piece he wrote for a man is the tiny "Italian singer's aria" in Act I of Rosenkavalier. It's supposed to poke fun at Italian tenors, but it's gorgeous in spite of itself. And nobody does it better than Pavarotti.

Act 2:

Sophie falls in love with Octavian when he delivers the silver rose. She has never wanted to be with Baron Ochs, but her father insists...

Act 3:

Thanks to a neat bit of "entrapment," Sophie's father sees what a womanizing oinker Baron Ochs is, and Pops blesses Sophies marriage to Octavian.

There's a famous movie of Rosenkavalier, starring Elizabeth Schwarzkopf. Personally, I couldn't help but notice (and notice and notice) the fact that Octavian—the boy—was a girl. That may work for some people, but I'm not one of them.

Tales of Hoffmann

Jacques Offenbach

Prologue:

Prologue:
Drunken poet Hoffmann tells everyone in the tavern about the women he has loved—and lost.

Act 1:

Hoffmann falls madly in love with Olympia. Unfortunately, she turns out to be a wind-up mechanical doll.

Act 2:

Hoffmann falls madly in love with the courtesan Giulietta, a Venetian blonde. Unfortunately, she steals his shadow—his <u>soul.</u>

Act 3:

Hoffmann falls madly in love with Antonia, a singer. Unfortunately, she sings herself to death.

Epilogue:

Hoffmann, story finished, gets falling-down drunk.

REAL Bottom Line: Despite serious flaws (e.g., musically and dramatically, Hoffmann is a spectator in his own story), Tales of Hoffmann is (in this dude's opionion) one of the half-dozen finest Operas ever written. And, as of the mid 1990s, we have two magnificent Hoffmanns (Placido Domingo & Neil Shicoff) both at the top of their game. Hear it! See it! Hum it!

TOSCA : *Giacomo Puccini*

SO, DID YOU HEAR? THERE'S AN ESCAPED PRISONER ON THE LOOSE.

HE'S BEEN WATCHING TOM SNYDER FOR 12 HOURS NOW, BUT WE CAN'T BREAK HIM...

Act 1:

Cavaradossi, painting a mural in church, pauses to hide Angelotti, an escaped political prisoner. Tosca, Cavaradossi's jealous girlfriend comes to church. So does Baron Scarpia.

The music that ends Act I (called the *"Te Deum"*) is one of the most brilliant strokes in Opera. Scarpia raves on in lip-licking lust (*"Ah, Tosca..."*), as the congregation prays and the nice church music plays.

Act 2:

Scarpia has Cavaradossi thrown into prison and tortured. Tosca says she'll give herself to Scarpia if he lets Cavaradossi go free. Lecherous old Scarpia gives her two safe-conduct passes to escape Rome, but instead of keeping her end of the bargain, she stabs him.

HEY...HOW COME MINE DIDN'T DO THAT...

Act 3:

Cavaradossi, who according to plan, was to face a "fake" execution, finds to his great surprise, that the bullets are real. He dies, so despondent Tosca kills herself.

150

La Traviata

Guiseppe Verdi

Act 1:

Alfredo, young dude from the suburbs, meets Violetta (Parisian courtesan), and they fall in love.

Act 2:

The lovers live out in the country. Violetta peddles her jewelry to support them. Alfredo's father comes to Violetta to beg her to end the affair (*he says that their relationship will prevent Alfredo's sister from marrying, but I'm not buying it!*). Violetta relents and, without explaining to Alfredo, she moves back to Paris alone. Alfredo, runs into her at a party and insults her and her escort. Alfredo's father arrives just in time to tell his son what a meathead he's been: *She did it for you, stupido!*

The Greta Garbo movie, *Camille,* was based on the same play that the Opera was taken from.

Act 3:

Alfredo returns to Violetta...but she dies from consumption. (Personally, I think she croaks from singing too many razzle dazzle arias. The role is so brutal that a Soprano who can sing the flashy coloratura in the first act is unlikely to have enough dramatic heft for the last act; and conversely, any sister hefty enough for the last act would probably be a klutz in the fancy-schmancy first act...)

151

Il Trovatore

Giuseppe Verdi

Act 1:

A Spanish lady (Leonora) loves Manrico, the "Troubadour." She throws herself into his arms but misses and ends up in the arms of Count di Luna, who also loves her. Manrico rushes off to swordfight with Mr. di Luna.

Act 2:

An old gypsy broad named Azucena announces to her buddies that, unbenownst to them, di Luna and Manrico are brothers. (Not *that* kind of brothers!) Leonora, having presumed that Manrico (a lover, not a fighter) was iced by di Luna, enlists in the Convent. When Manrico learns that 1) Leonora is in a Convent and 2) his Prince is being attacked, he rushes off to 3) save his Prince from the Bad Guys and 4) save Leonora from the Nuns.

Di Luna, waiting at the Convent, sings such a beautiful aria (*Il balen*) that it's hard for us civilians to think he's a bad guy.

Manrico arrives at the last second and "spirits Leonora away."

Act 3:

Azucena, Manrico's foster-mom, is captured.

Manreek tries to rescue her but the inept fool is captured too.

Act 4:

Leonora offers herself to di Luna if he'll free Manrico. Di Luna digs that, but Leonora outsmarts him (?) by poisoning herself. Di Luna kills Manrico, then learns (oy vay) that Manrico was his brother.

LEONORA

MANRICO

BROTHER

This is the Opera that Groucho, Chico, and Manrico Marx butchered in their totally insane movie, *A Night at the Opera*.

THE RING OF THE NIBELUNG

Richard Wagner

Opera 1 — DAS RHEINGOLD (Prologue)

Bottom Line: Wotan, chairman of the gods, has made so many shifty deals that they're starting to catch up with him.

Scene 1:

Alberich, an ugly dwarf, steals gold guarded by the Rhine maidens, three young ladies who live under the Rhine River (in Germany, dudes).

Scene 2:

Wotan and his nagging wife Fricka argue about the castle (Valhalla) being built for them by two giants. Fricka's sister, Freia, the goddess of youth, is to be traded for the castle—which means that the gods'll get old. The giants say they'll accept the Rheingold instead of Freia, _if_ they get it by that night.

Scene 3 & 4:

Wotan and Loge, the god of fire, trick Alberich and take the gold to pay for the castle.

Opera 2 — DIE WALKURE

Bottom Line: The best and most melodic Opera of the bunch.

Act 1:

Siegmund falls in love with Sieglinde, his sister, who is married to Hunding, who aint too fond of visitors fondling his wife. So Sig and Sis run away.

153

Act 2:

Fricka, the goddess of nagging wives, bitches out Wotan for whoring around (Sigmund is his son) and disrespecting marriage. Wotan commands Brunnhilde (one of the nine warrior daughters of Erda the Earth Goddess and Wotan—the man got around) not to help the lovers (Fricka's orders), but Brunnhilde saves the pregnant Sieglinde. (Psst! Fricka can't stand Brunnhilde because, one, she's in-your-face proof of Wotan's whoring, and two, she's Wotan's favorite daughter.)

WHERE'S MY MASTER?

SORRY PAL, I PUT HE TO SLEEP...

Act 3:

For disobeying him, Wotan puts Brunnhilde to sleep and surrounds her with fire so that only a fearless stud can save her. (*That's* what <u>happens</u>; *this* is what it <u>feels like</u>: Two people stand on a rock shouting for 20 minutes, then, just as you're about to doze off, Wagner hits you with the most beautiful music imaginable...the music fills you with a sense of your own divinity, lifts you right out of your seat...)

Opera 3 # SIEGFRIED

Bottom Line: Siegfried the hero is even dumber than Manrico (the bubble-head from Il Trovatore).

Act 1:

Siegfried, son of Siegmund and Sieglinde (Wagner was clearly from the George Foreman school of naming), is raised by a dwarf named Mime until the day Sig sings a big song about his Magic Sword.

Act 2:

Siegfried kills a dragon and takes the dragon's Magic Ring.

Act 3:

Siegfried finds Brunnhilde asleep on her fiery rock. When he awakes her, Brunnhilde, once a warrior goddess, is now a mortal woman in love with a dummy with a sword.

GOTTERDAMMERUNG

Prologue:

The gods wait at Valhalla for the end. Siegfried marries Brunnhilde by giving her his Magic Ring. (He keeps his Bat Man Wristwatch for himself?)

Act 1:

Hagen and Gunther (bad guys) plot to get the Magic Ring by giving Siggy a Magic Potion that'll make him forget Brunnhilde and fall in lust with Gutrune (Gunther's sister). Sig, who is tough but none too bright, comes sailing down the Rhine right into their trap, drinks the Magic Potion, has a little guilt-free sex with Gutrune ("I swear, Brunnhilde, they drugged me.") Siegfried, who is no dumber without a memory than he was when he had one, goes off to bring back Brunnhilde and the Ring for Gunther.

Act 2:

Siggy returns with Brunnhilde and the Magic Ring. She denounces everybody.

Act 3:

Hagen kills Siegfried, Brunnhilde joins Siegfried on the burning funeral pyre and sings her glorious buns off, the Rhinebimbos get the Magic Ring, fire destroys the gods...and, well, that about does it.

Bottom Line: **Four Operas, lasting some 20 hours, are exhausting, irritating, pretentions, and vaaaaaaay too long, but you have no doubt that you've witnessed one of the greatest works of art by anyone anywhere ever.**

P.S.—Wagner wrote his own long-winded librettos for all of his Operas/Music-Dramas.

Certain CALLS

The Intellectual Approach

Since I have poked fun at the intellectual approach to Opera, you might be surprised that I am now going to give you a pitch on behalf of it. Examining in detail all or part of an Opera, or of Opera in general; learning in-depth the difference between Opera Seria and Wagner's symphonic Music Dramas; studying composers or periods or libretti (now that we're getting fancy, we may as well spell the plural the right way); or any of that other "stuff" I have teasingly called the "intellectual approach" to Opera—especially learning another language or two—I now say, "Go for it!" When you reach the point when you want to examine any aspect of Opera, go for it! The intellectual approach is great when you're doing it from the heart.

Which brings us to Mr. Wagner's Ring Cycle.

After all the ragging I did, maybe you think I don't like Wagner's Ring. I think it's one of the greatest works ever created by any human in any field ever. Nothing in Opera rewards the intellectual approach more than Wagner's Ring. Go for it!

And if, by the way, you think that I'm trying to persuade you to believe that Mozart is an overrated turkey, think again: I don't want you to follow me or anyone else; get in touch with your own soul. Follow your own tastes.

BOTTOM LINE: USE ZEALOTS AND FANATICS LIKE STAFAN ZUCKER, WAGNER, AND ME TO BROADEN YOUR ARENA OF ECSTACY, NOT TO NARROW IT.

The Future of Opera

As the author of a book on Opera, I should say a word about modern Opera, even though as a passionate listener, I'd say that Opera pretty much croaked after Richard Strauss. (Excuse me—I hear the Opera Police banging on my door again.) After the 1920s, other composers took Opera in directions that many listeners simply didn't dig. <u>Wozzeck</u> (1925) and <u>Lulu</u> (1935), by **Alban Berg** (1885-1935), were atonal Operas that, depending upon your point of view, either enlarged the repetory, or were forced down Opera lovers' throats. Czechoslovakian composer **Leos Janacek** (1854-1928) wrote several Operas, the most popular of which was <u>Jenufa</u> (1903). <u>Peter Grimes</u> (1945) and <u>Billy Budd</u> (1951), by British composer **Benjamin Britten** (1913-1976), are some people's cup of tea, and others not. **Gian Carlo Menotti** (b.1911), an Italian who's spent most of his life in America, is probably the most successful composer of "American" Operas, including <u>Amahl and the Night Visitors</u> (1951) and <u>The Medium</u> (1946). The ragtime Opera <u>Treemonisha</u> (1915) by **Scott Joplin** (1868-1917) hasn't had much luck, whereas <u>Porgy and Bess</u> (1935) by **George Gershwin** (1898-1937) has had more than it deserves. <u>Nixon in China</u>, a contemporary Opera by **John Adams** (1947), was a fair success. However.

I seriously doubt that the future of Opera lies in any of those directions. The future of Opera probably lies in its past—in tomorrow's Pavarotti or Callas.

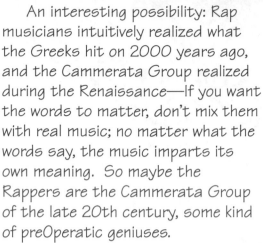

An interesting possibility: Rap musicians intuitively realized what the Greeks hit on 2000 years ago, and the Cammerata Group realized during the Renaissance—If you want the words to matter, don't mix them with real music; no matter what the words say, the music imparts its own meaning. So maybe the Rappers are the Cammerata Group of the late 20th century, some kind of preOperatic geniuses.

My view of Opera's ideal future: I'd love to see "real" singers like LaBelle and Streisand and Stevie Wonder and Whitney Huston and Boyz 2 Men and Tony Bennet and beautiful BeBop Betty Carter singing Opera from the soul, taking Rossini's advice all the way to the edge and singing however their individual bebop souls tell them to sing it. I can hear LaBelle singing Isolde. And Stevie Wonder riffing from one aria to another (and wouldn't Michael Jackson make one hell of a Madam Butterfly?).

...and then Domingo would hear Stevie's wonderful riffing and El Placido would loosen up and get down...

...and after hearing Michael Jackson's heartbreaking Butterfly, Pavarotti would record <u>Luigi di Lammermoor</u> and Bellini's <u>Norman</u>...

Epilogue

What does OPERA **mean** TO ME?

Sometimes I feel like my emotions are too big for the neighborhood I live in. The world is too sane, too Noah's arky ("...and on this ark, you will put one job, one wife, one personality, one hobby, one emotion, one favorite team, one best friend...one, one, one!!!).

Screw <u>one</u>! I want to experience <u>everything</u> life has to offer.
I want Life with a capital **L** and a small L and everything in between.
I want to be as strong and fast and smart as I can be. I want to be Air Amadeus Leontyne Coltrane Sugar Ray Shakespeare. I want the courage to risk a good ass-whippin' for something I believe in and to love without holding back. I want to tell the truth, I want to lie, I want to be a saint, I want to make love twenty-four hours a day—I want everything life has to offer, as long and as strong and as often as I can take it. And if death has anything, I want that too!

That, mother-thumpers, is what Opera means to me.

DISCOGRAPHY

BELLINI	NORMA	◆(Intensely Emotional) Callas, Ludwig, Corelli. Serrafin—EMI.
		◆(Purely Musical) Sutherland, Horne, Alexander, Cross. Bonynge—London.
	I PURITANI	◆Callas, di Stefano, Panerai, Rossi-Lemeni. *Serafin*—Angel.
BIZET	CARMEN	◆Callas, Gedda. *Pretre.*
		◆My hard-to-find favorite: Conchita Supervia & Jose Luccioni. 1930s)
DONIZETTI	ELIXIR OF LOVE	◆Either Pavarotti recording—with Joan Sutherland or Kathleen Battle.
	LUCIA DI LAMMERMOOR	◆Callas, di Stefano, Gobbi. *Serafin*—Seraphim
GOUNOD	FAUST	◆Freni, Domingo, Allen, Ghiaurov. *Pretre*—London.
HANDEL	RINALDO	◆Horne, Gasdia, Weidinger, Palacio. *Fisher*—Nuova Era.
LEONCAVALLO	PAGLIACCI	◆It's a Tenor's Opera, so go with your favorite
MASCAGNI	CAVALLERIA RUSTICIANA	◆Callas/di Stefano
		◆DelMonaco/Suliotis
		◆Bjorling/Tebaldi
MASSANET	MANON	◆(French Style) Sills, Gedda, Souzay, Bacquier. *Rudel*—Angel.
		◆Italian Style) Freni, Pavarotti, Panerai. *Maaq*—Verona.
MOZART	ABDUCTION FROM SERAGLIO	◆Auger, Grist, Schreier, Moll. *Bohm*—DG
	DON GIOVANNI	◆Schwarzkopf, Welitsch, Gobbi, Dermota. *Furtwangler*—Olympic.
		◆Rethberg, Helletsgruber, Bokor, Borgioli, Lazzari, Pinza. *Walter*—Melodram
	MAGIC FLUTE	◆Berger, Lemnitz, Beilke, Roswaenge, Husch. *Beecham*—Nimbus, 1938.
MUSSORGSKY	BORIS GODUNOV	◆Lear, Lanigan, Christoff. *Cluytens*—Angel.
OFFENBACH	TALES OF HOFFMANN	◆Either Placido Domingo (DG) or Neil Shicoff (Angel).
PUCCINI	LA BOHEME	◆Freni, Pavarotti, Panerai. *Karajan.*—London.
	LA FANCIULLA DEL WEST	◆Tebaldi, Del Monaco, MacNeil, Tozzi. *Capuana*—London.
	MADAM BUTTERFLY	◆Price, Tucker. *Leinsdorf*—RCA..
	MANON LESCAUT	◆Albanese, Bjorling, Merrill. *Perlea*—RCA Gold Seal.
	TOSCA	◆Callas, di Stefano, Gobbi. *De Sabata*—EMI.

RESPHIGI	**L**A **F**IAMMA	
	(odd Opera)	◆Tokody,Takacs, Kelen, Solyom-Naby. *Gardelli—* Hungariton.
ROSSINI	**B**ARBER OF **S**EVILLE	◆Capsir, Borgioli, Stracciari. *Molajoli—Columbia, 1929.*
	L'ITALIANA IN **A**LGIERI	◆Horne, Battle, Palacio, Ramey, Zaccaria. *Scimone—* Erato.
	OTELLO	◆Von Stade, Carreras, Ramey. *Lopez-Cobos—Phillips.*
	SEMIRAMIDE	◆Studer, Larmoe, Lopardo, Ramey. *Marin—DG.*
STRAUSS	**G**UNTRAM	
	(odd Opera)	◆Tokody, Reiner Goldberg [what a Tenor!], Solyom-Nagi, Gatti. *Queller—CBS*
	ROSENKAVALIER	◆Schwarzkopf, Stich-Randall, Ludwig, Edelman. *Karajan:*
VERDI	**A**IDA	◆Price, Bumbry, Domingo, Milnes, Raimondi. *Leinsdorf—* RCA.
		◆Callas, Dominguez, Del Monaco. *DeFabritis—live* Mexico City, 1951.
	ERNANI	◆Price [She'll kill you!], Bergonzi, Sereni. *Schippers—* RCA.
	RIGOLETTO	◆Callas, di Stefano, Gobbi. *Serafin—EMI.*
	LA **T**RAVIATA	◆Go with your favorite Soprano—Callas, Albanese, Sills, Sutherland, Moffo...
	IL **T**ROVATORE	◆Plowright, Fassbender, Domingo, Zacanaro. *Giulini—* DG.
WAGNER	**P**ARSIFAL	◆Modl, Windgassen, London, Weber. *Knappertsbusch—* TelDec, 1951.
	THE **M**ASTER**S**INGER	◆Janowitz, Fassbaender, Konya, Unger, Stewart. Kubelik—NYTO, 1969.

THE COMPLETE "RING" CYCLE

	DAS **R**HEINGOLD	◆Modl, Konetzi, Jurinac, Grummer, Cavelti, Malaniuk,
	DIE **W**ALKURE	Klose, Suthaus, Windgassen, Patzak, Frantz, Frick,
	SIEGFRIED	Neidlinger. *Furtwangler—Angel.*
	GOTTERDAMMERUNG	

RESOURCES

Schwann "Opus" catalogue, available at any record store, lists virtually every Tape, CD, and Recording currently in print. Video catalogues are available at any large Video outlet. Most of the big labels are available in large record stores, but if you have trouble finding them, you can order them directly from the addresses and phone numbers below:

Allegro Imports
3434 S.E. Milwaukie Ave.
Portland, OR 97202
(503) 232-4213

Angel-EMI
810 Seventh Ave., 4th Floor
New York, NY 10019
(212) 603-4167

Kultur
121 Hwy. 36
W. Long Branch,
NJ 07764
(800) 458-5887

Nimbus
P.O. Box 7427
Charlottesville, VA 22906
(804) 985-1100

Polygram Classics
Worldwide Plaza
825 Eighth Ave.
New York, NY 10010

RCA/BMG Classics
1133 Ave. of the Americas
New York, NY 10036
(212) 930-4000

Sony Classical/CBS
1285 Ave. of
the Americas
New York, NY 10019
(212) 445-4763

V.I.E.W. Video
34 East 23rd St.
New York, NY 10019
(800) 843-9843

For all things Wagnerian, write: **Wagner Society of New York,** P.O. Box 949, Ansonia Station, New York, NY 10023-0949.

For access to collector's Tapes, CDs, Records, and Videos, the most interesting place I've found is Stefan Zucker's Bel Canto Society. Here is a brief sample of what's available—along with an address you can write to for either a Catalogue or Information.

Opera Fanatic's Catalogue
Bel Canto Society
11 Riverside Drive
New York, NY 10023
(800) 347-5056

GLOSSARY

Aria	A "song" from an Opera; it may either stop the action or advance it.
Arioso	Slightly melodic; partway between Aria and Recitativo; doesn't stop the action.
Bel canto	(It., Beautiful singing) A 19th century school of singing/composing; the Operas of Rossini, Donizetti & Bellini
Claque	(F.) People hired to applaud one singer and/or boo another.
Coloratura	The most florid and technically demanding kind of singing; the term usually refers to a Soprano, but it can apply to any voice category
Diva	(It., goddess) An over-the-edge term for your favorite soprano.
Fioritura	(It., flowering) Vocal embellishments that singers (or composers) add to an Aria.
Intermezzo	Music written for the middle of an act, usually indicating the passage of time.
Legato	(It., connected) A musical direction to tie the notes smoothly together
Leitmotif	A short tune representing characters or ideas, that reached its pinnacle in Wagner's Operas.
Libretto	(It., little book) The text or words of an Opera.
Lieder	(G., songs) German "art" songs, usually sung by Opera singers.
Music Drama	To Wagner, Opera was a series of action-stopping musical numbers; Wagner's ideal was the perfect non-stop unity of Words & Music—which he called Music drama.
Opera buffa	(It., comic Opera) It's supposed to make you laugh.
Opera comique	A French term, usually referring to "Operas" with spoken Dialogue between Arias.
Opera seria	(It., serious Opera) It's not supposed to make you laugh...but sometimes it does.
Operetta	It has lighter music and is non-Italian (e.g., Viennese Operetta & Gilbert & Sullivan)
Oratorio	A religious, Opera-like composition with no action: the singers just sing.
Overture	A piece of instrumental music (usually about ten minutes long) played before the Opera.
Recitative	The talk-like part of the Opera between Arias, Duets, etc.—esp. in early Opera
Singspiel	(G., singing play) A German "working class" Opera with spoken dialogue.
Spinto	A voice with more brilliance and power than the lighter "lyric" Soprano or Tenor, yet not as robust as the "dramatic" Soprano or Tenor.
Squillo	(It., ring [as in a bell]) The voice's penetrating power and "ping." If a voice sends a shiver up your spine and gives you chills, it has "squillo."
Stacatto	The opposite of Legato—each note is hit quickly and separately (like left-jabs).
Trill	The rapid alteration of two separate notes—a fancy Bel canto trick.
Verismo	Naturalistic Opera, often violent (*Cav & Pag*), sometimes not (*La Boheme*).

BIBLIOGRAPHY

Barber, David W. **WHEN THE FAT LADY SINGS.** Toronto, Canada: Sound and Vision, 1990.

Blyth, Alan. **OPERA ON CD.** London: Kyle Kathie Ltd, 1992.

DiGaetani, John Louis. **AN INVITATION TO THE OPERA.** New York: Anchor Books, 1986.

Ehrlich, Scott. **PAUL ROBESON: ATHLETE, ACTOR, SINGER, ACTIVIST.** Los Angeles: Melrose Sq. Pub.,1988.

Englander, Roger. **OPERA: WHAT'S ALL THE SCREAMING ABOUT?** New York: Walker and Co., 1983.

Koestenbaum, Wayne. **THE QUEEN'S THROAT.** New York: Vintage Books, 1993.

Lebrecht, Norman. **THE BOOK OF MUSICAL ANECDOTES.** New York: The Free Press, 1985.

Lynch, Stacy Combs. **CLASSICAL MUSIC FOR BEGINNERS.** New York: Writers & Readers Pub., 1994.

Kolodin, Irving. **THE OPERA OMNIBUS.** Canada: Clark, Irwin & Company Limited, 1976.

McCourt, James. **MAWRDEW CZGOWCHWZ.** New York: The Noonday Press, 1971.

Mordden, Ethan. **OPERA ANECDOTES.** New York: Oxford University Press, 1985.

Pavarotti, Luciano and Wright, William. **PAVAROTTI: MY OWN STORY.** New York: Warner Books, 1981.

Rice, Anne. **CRY TO HEAVEN.** New York: Pinnacle Books, 1982.

Rosenthal, H. & Warrack, J. **THE CONCISE OXFORD DICTIONARY OF OPERA.** Oxford: Oxford U. .Press, 1980.

Simon, Henry W. **100 GREAT OPERAS AND THEIR STORIES.** New York: Dolphin Books, 1960.

Steane, J.B. **VOICES: SINGERS & CRITICS.** Portland, Oregon: Amadeus Press, 1992.

Stroff, Stephen. **OPERA: AN INFORMAL GUIDE.** Chicago: a cappella books, 1992.

Walsh, Michael. **WHO'S AFRAID OF CLASSICAL MUSIC?** New York: Fireside Books, 1989.

PERIODICALS

OPERA FANATIC: The Magazine for Lovers of Expressive Singing. Bel Canto Society. New York

OPERA NEWS. The Metropolitan Opera Guild. New York.

OPERA QUARTERLY. Duke University Press. Durham, North Carolina

OTHER

SCHWANN OPUS. Reference Guide to Classical Music. Santa Fe, New Mexico. Fall 1995.

INDEX

Abduction from the Seraglio
(Mozart), 26
Adams, John, 157
African American opera
singers, 122
Aida (Verdi), 36, 127
Alceste (Gluck), 24
Alcina (Handel), 21
Amahl and the Night Visitors
(Menotti), 157
Anderson, Marian, 86, 92
Andromeda (Manelli), 62
Anna Bolena (Donizetti), 33
aria, 19, 65
Ariadne auf Naxos (R.
Strauss), 52

Barber of Seville, The
(Rossini), 29, 32, 128
baritones, 61, 71
bassos, 61, 71
Bayreuth opera house, 41
Beethoven, Ludwig van, 30, 38
Bel Canto, 28–34
Bellini, Vincenzo, 34
Berg, Alban, 157
Berlioz, Hector, 45
Billy Budd (Britten), 157
Bing, Rudolf, 92
Bizet, Georges, 46
Bjoerling, Jussi, 91, 113–14
Bluebeard's Castle (Bartok),
129
Bohème, La (Puccini), 50, 130
Boito, Arrigo, 136

Boris Godunov
(Mussorgsky), 49, 131
Borodin, Alexander, 49
Britten, Benjamin, 157

Callas, Maria, 87–90, 92
Camerata Group, 16
Carmen (Bizet), 46, 132
Carreras, José, 98
Caruso, Enrico, 76–80
castrati, 62–67
Cavalleria Rusticana
(Mascagni), 47–48, 133
Cavalli, Pietro Francesco, 63
Cesti, Marc' Antonio, 63
Chaliapin, Feodor, 84
Charpentier, Marc-Antoine,
46
Cherubini, Luigi, 43
church music, 14–15
Cinderella (Rossini), 29
Clemenza di Tito, La
(Mozart), 27
coloratura sopranos, 61, 73
Corelli, Franco, 93
Così Fan Tutte (Mozart), 27
critics, music, 106
Daughter of the Regiment
(Donizetti), 33
Del Monaco, Mario, 94
De Reszke, Jean, 75
Dido and Aeneas (Purcell),
20
di Stefano, Giuseppe, 90
divas, 74–75
Domingo, Placido, 97
Don Carlos (Verdi), 36
Don Giovanni (Mozart), 27,
134
Donizetti, Gaetano, 33
Donzelli, Domenico, 70
Duprez, Gilbert-Louis, 69–70

Egyptian music, 10–11
Electra (R. Strauss), 52
Elixir of Love, The (Donizetti),
33, 135
English opera, 20–22
Ernani (Verdi), 36

Eugene Onegin (Tchaikovsky),
49
Euridice (Peri & Rinuccini), 17

Falstaff (Verdi), 37
Fanciulla del West (Puccini),
50
Farinelli (castrato), 66
Farrar, Geraldine, 81
Faust (Gounod), 44, 136
Fedora (Giordano), 77
Ferri (castrato), 65
Fidelio (Beethoven), 38
fioritura, 73
Flagstad, Kirsten, 85
Fledermaus (J. Strauss),
137
Fliegende Hollander, Der
(Wagner), 40
Forza del Destino (Verdi), 36
Freischütz, Der (Weber), 38
French opera, 43–46

Galli-Curci, Amelita, 82
Garcia, Manuel, 68
Garden, Mary, 81
German opera, 23–27,
38–42, 52–55, 72,
104–6
Gershwin, George, 157
Gigli, Benjamino, 83
Giordano, Umberto, 77
Glinka, Mikhail, 49
Gluck, Christoph Willibald,
23–24

Melba, Nellie, 75
Melchior, Lauritz, 85
Menotti, Gian Carlo, 157
Mephistophele (Boito), 136
Messa di Gloria (Rossini), 32
Meyerbeer, Giacomo, 44, 73
mezzo sopranos, 61, 73
Monteverdi, Claudio, 18, 63
Moses in Egypt (Rossini), 29, 32
Mozart, Wolfgang Amadeus, 25–27, 53–54
Mussorgsky, Modest, 49
Muzio, Claudia, 84

Nabucco (Verdi), 36
Nilsson, Birgit, 94
Nixon in China (Adams), 157
Norma (Bellini), 34, 143
Norman, Jessye, 96
Nourrit, Adolphe, 69

Oberon (Weber), 38
Offenbach, Jacques, 44
opera
    all-time favorites, 123–55
    characteristic features of, 4–8
    learning to appreciate, 1–3, 101–7, 124, 156, 159
    origins of, 10–21, 62
    present and future of, 157–58
    summaries of plots, 127–55
Opera Buffa, 27
opera houses, 17–18, 41, 90
Opera Seria, 27
opera singers, 57–99, 107–20
    African American, 122
    all-time favorites, 117–20
    audience reactions to, 5–6
    ethnicity of, 111–12
    gender of, 62–68
    pop and jazz singers as, 108–10, 158
    role of, in shaping opera, 19, 55
Orfeo (Monteverdi & Striggio), 18
Orfeo ed Euridice (Gluck), 24
Otello (Rossini), 29, 32
Otello (Verdi), 37

Gobbi, Tito, 90
Götterdämmerung (Wagner), 41, 155
Gounod, Charles, 44
Greek drama, 10–12

Handel, George Frideric, 21–22
Hofmannsthal, Hugo von, 53
Horne, Marilyn, 96
Huguenots, Les (Meyerbeer), 44, 138

Idomeneo (Mozart), 27
Incoronazione di Poppea, L' (Monteverdi), 18
Italian Girl in Algiers, The (Rossini), 29, 32
Italian opera, 7–8, 16–20, 28–37, 47–48, 50–51, 72, 104–6
Italian sob, 69

Janácek, Leos, 157
Jenufa (Janácek), 157
Jeritza, Maria, 84
Joplin, Scott, 157

Lablache, Luigi, 71
La Scala opera house, 90
Lauri-Volpi, Giacomo, 84
Lehmann, Lotte, 85
Leider, Frida, 85

Leoncavallo, Ruggiero, 48
Lind, Jenny, 73
Lohengrin (Wagner), 40
Lombardi (Verdi), 36
Louise (Charpentier), 46
Lucia di Lammermoor (Donizetti), 33, 139
Lully, Jean-Baptiste, 43, 44
Lulu (Berg), 157

Macbeth (Verdi), 36
Madame Butterfly (Puccini), 50, 140
Magic Flute, The (Mozart), 26, 141
Malibran, Maria, 71
Manelli, Francesco, 62
Manon (Massenet), 44, 142
Manon Lescaut (Puccini), 50, 142
Maria Stuarda (Donizetti), 33
Marriage of Figaro, The (Mozart), 27
Martinelli, Giovanni, 83
Mascagni, Pietro, 47–48
masques, 20
Massenet, Jules, 44
McCormack, John, 82
Medea (Cherubini), 43
Medium, The (Menotti), 157
Meistersinger von Nürnberg, Die (Wagner), 40

Pagliacci (Leoncavallo), 48, 144
Parsifal (Wagner), 40
Pasta, Giuditta, 71
Patti, Adelina, 74
Pavarotti, Luciano, 97
Peri, Jacopo, 17
Pertile, Aureliano, 84
Peter Grimes (Britten), 145, 157
Pinza, Ezio, 84, 116
Ponselle, Rosa, 86
Porgy and Bess (Gershwin), 146, 157
Price, Leontyne, 95, 115
Prophète, Le (Meyerbeer), 44
Puccini, Giacomo, 50–51
Purcell, Henry, 20
Puritani, I (Bellini), 34

Quem Queritis plays, 15

recitativo, 19, 28
Renaissance music, 15–17
Rheingold, Das (Wagner), 41, 153
Rigoletto (Verdi), 36, 147
Rimsky-Korsakov, Nikolai, 49
Rinaldo (Handel), 21
Ring Cycle (Wagner), 40–41, 153–55

Rinuccini, Ottavio, 17
Ritorno d'Ulisse, Il (Monteverdi), 18
Roberto Devereux (Donizetti), 33
Robeson, Paul, 111
Roman drama, 13
Roméo et Juliet (Gounod), 44
Rosenkavalier, Der (R. Strauss), 52, 64, 148
Rossini, Gioacchino, 29–32
Rubini, Giovanni, 69
Ruffo, Titta, 81
Russian opera, 49

Salieri, Antonio, 26
Salome (R. Strauss), 52
Samson (Handel), 21
Schipa, Tito, 84
Schorr, Friedrich, 85
Schröder-Devrient, Wilhemine, 72
Schumann-Heink, Ernestine, 82
Schwartzkopf, Elisabeth, 94
Semiramide (Rossini), 29, 32, 64
Siegfried (Wagner), 41, 154
Sills, Beverly, 96
Singspiel, 26
Slavic opera, 49
Somnambula, La (Bellini), 34
Sontag, Henriette, 73
sopranos, 61, 71–75
Strauss, Johann, 137
Strauss, Richard, 52–53

Supervia, Conchita, 84
Sutherland, Joan, 95

Tales of Hoffmann, The (Offenbach), 44, 64, 149
Tamburini, Antonio, 71
Tancredi (Rossini), 29, 64
Tannhäuser (Wagner), 40
Tauber, Richard, 86
Tchaikovsky, Peter, 49
Tebaldi, Renata, 93
tenors, 61, 67–71
Tosca (Puccini), 50, 150
Traviata, La (Verdi), 36, 151
Treemonisha (Joplin), 157
Tristan und Isolde (Wagner), 40
Trittico (Puccini), 50
trouser roles, 63–64
Trovatore, Il (Verdi), 36, 152
Troyens, Les (Berlioz), 45
Tucker, Richard, 93
Turandot (Puccini), 50
Turk in Italy, The (Rossini), 29
twentieth century opera, 50–53, 157

Verdi, Giuseppe, 35–37, 107
Verismo, 46–48
Viardot-Garcia, Pauline, 73
vibrato, 69
Viennese opera, 23–27
voices, categories of, 60–61

Wagner, Richard, 38–42, 121
Walküre, Die (Wagner), 41, 153–54
Weber, Carl Maria von, 38
Werther (Massenet), 44
William Tell (Rossini), 29, 69
Wozzeck (Berg), 157

BIOS

RON DAVID

Ron David is a writer, editor, husband, lover, father, weightlifting basketball player, member of RAWI [Radius of Arab-American Writers] who has not yet visited Lebanon although both sets of his grandparents were born there. Ronaldo David has written two other Beginners books [ARABS & ISRAEL FOR BEGINNERS and JAZZ FOR BEGINNERS and is currently at work on TONI MORRISON FOR BEGINNERS]. He has also written four novels, one of which [THE AUTAOBIOGRAPHY OF ARIEL SHARON] was awarded a fellowship from the New Jersey Council on the Arts.

Ron is living happily ever after with Susan, an artist/writer who is currently in-training to kick Mike Tyson's butt. (She'll last longer than McNeely!)

PAUL GORDON

Paul Gordon is an artist and designer living at the foot of the Williamsburg Bridge in Brooklyn, NY. He is the illustrator of three other Beginners books on Martin Heidegger, Noam Chomsky, and William Shakespeare. Paul likes Opera, loves Jazz and is grateful to have contributed to anything Ron David has written.